Councils of
Churches and the
Ecumenical
Vision

Councils of Churches and the Ecumenical Vision

**Diane Kessler &
Michael Kinnamon**

Risk
BOOK SERIES

WCC Publications, Geneva

Cover design: Rob Lucas

ISBN 2-8254-1324-0

© 2000, WCC Publications, World Council of Churches
150 route de Ferney, P.O. Box 2100
1211 Geneva 2, Switzerland
Website: http://www.wcc-coe.org

Risk Book Series no. 90

Printed in Switzerland

To the memory of
Marlin VanElderen
editor, ecumenical colleague, friend,
brother in Christ

Table of Contents

Introduction

This book is about councils of churches and the people who are part of them. It is written from an American perspective, with which the authors are most familiar. The situation in the United States is perhaps unique in the number and diversity of state, regional and local councils of churches within its borders. Forty-seven states have councils, and within those states at least sixty metropolitan ecumenical bodies and over a thousand regional and local councils are in operation.

At the same time, we are mindful of other regional and local ecumenical endeavours, such as in the United Kingdom where the "Churches Together" model has stimulated community-based ecumenical organizing. We have sought to name contexts other than our own in the text. We also realize that an intimate knowledge of these ecumenical bodies is not possible for us. Yet ecumenical theory applies equally to all, and we hope that this book will stimulate reflection about each situation.

We have talked with many colleagues involved in conciliar ecumenism. Sometimes they are wrestling with the inevitable stumbling blocks that accompany any ecumenical enterprise. Ecumenical leaders also have voiced a need – indeed, a hunger – to comprehend more clearly the vision that grounds and shapes councils of churches. They have worked to make connections between theory and practice. Thus, we have begun and ended this book in chapters 1 and 10 with the big picture – the vision of and challenges for the future of the whole ecumenical movement.

In the heart of this text, however, we have focused particularly on councils of churches. How do councils look when they correspond to the ecumenical vision? What qualities are desirable in volunteer and professional ecumenical leaders? What are the spiritual marks and fruits of ecumenical commitment? In what ways should councils address the relationship between Christian churches and people of other faiths? Because of the evolving nature of leadership in the ecumenical movement, a steady stream of new professional and volunteer leaders keep raising these questions. These are the issues we have sought to address in this book. We hope the ideas expressed here will be another means to keep the ecumenical tradition alive and growing.

Participation in the ecumenical movement is stimulating, energizing and challenging. It can be frustrating, but the rewards are greater than one can imagine or anticipate, because the ecumenical calling is at the heart of the gospel and is the very essence of the triune God.

We have enjoyed this collaborative effort. We are grateful to the World Council of Churches, whose members have been addressing these issues since the WCC's formation, for publishing this text.

We pray that this book will help in the ongoing process of calling Christians to reframe their picture. Shared life is the *norm*. Division demands explanation.

In the name of the One who calls us to be One.

MICHAEL KINNAMON   DIANE C. KESSLER

1. The Vision of the Ecumenical Movement

A council of churches, as we are using the term in this book, may be defined as a voluntary association of separated and autonomous Christian churches, within a defined geographic area, through which its members seek to manifest their fellowship with one another, to engage in common activities of witness and service, and to advance towards the goal of visible unity. A council of churches can be distinguished from a temporary coalition in that its members make an enduring commitment to one another. As the delegates to the first assembly of the World Council of Churches (Amsterdam 1948) put it: "We intend to stay together." A council of churches can be distinguished from a clergy association or Christian service organization in that its members are not committed individuals but churches. A council of churches can be distinguished from an interfaith council in that its self-understanding is explicitly shaped by the gospel of God's gracious love made known in Jesus Christ.

Councils of this sort, as we will show more fully in the next chapter, are a new thing in the history of the church. They are also crucial expressions and instruments of the modern ecumenical movement. While councils are not the unity for which Christ prayed or of which Paul writes, they *are* a major step beyond the competitive, antagonistic separation that has marked so much of Christian history.

Today, however, councils in many places are experiencing hard times. Whenever a church faces financial difficulties, support for ecumenical bodies is often quickly cut (an indication that councils are seen as external to the churches' "real identity and mission"). The staff members of many councils speak of the contradictory attitudes held by the member churches. "On the one hand, churches believe they should pass over to councils only a very small fraction of their work and a strictly limited mandate. On the other hand, those same churches expect more service from the council than it is possible to give" – especially in the face of diminished financial support.

An even more basic problem is succinctly named by Victor Hayward who, in the early 1970s, was responsible for relationships between the WCC and national councils of churches. After visiting nearly every national council on the planet (!), Hayward reached this conclusion:

> The key issue is that most churches show only partial commitment to what is involved in being a fellowship of churches. Where there is commitment, it is often to the council as an institution and not to the other churches that comprise its membership. Most councils, thus, are an ecumenical facade behind which churches remain as unecumenical as ever.

A great problem facing the ecumenical movement, writes veteran David Gill, is "the notion that churches, having demonstrated that their hearts are in the right place by joining an ecumenical body, can now leave ecumenism to the council and get on with denominational business-as-usual". Councils thus become "alibis", instruments for protecting denominational prerogatives. It is no wonder that many of them are struggling to maintain vitality and to articulate a clearer sense of purpose and direction.

In the pages that follow, we hope to address some of these issues directly – by recalling what the ecumenical movement, at its best, has said about councils of churches and by suggesting implications for the fellowship and ministry of these important bodies. We believe, however, that beneath any of the concerns raised above is the fundamental need for "vision". At the time of this writing, the WCC is considering major organizational changes. But "no institutional reform will be successful", argues the Council's general secretary, Konrad Raiser, "unless it is accompanied and guided by the effort to clarify and reaffirm the ecumenical vision". Churches involved in the ecumenical movement pay lip service to their oneness in Christ; but it is hard to deny that the exhilarating vision of earlier generations has given way, in many quarters, to what Albert Outler once called "an ecumenism of the status quo". "For my generation," wrote the WCC's first general secretary, Willem Visser 't Hooft, "the ecumenical movement had all the attraction of something unexpected and extraordinary. For the present generation it is simply part of the church's design." Every movement must find institutional forms if it is to be sustained; but if those forms lose touch with the movement's initial calling, they will surely stagnate, if not die.

Thus, we begin this exploration of councils of churches by setting forth what we understand to be the vision that has animated the ecumenical movement throughout the 20th century. The movement has undergone significant changes in its participants and priorities. But, as we see it, there is an underlying coherence rooted appropriately in the gospel.

It would be a miracle, of course, if all persons involved in ecumenical work agreed with our presentation. Our understanding of ecumenism is naturally shaped by our context and backgrounds, including the fact that we are both Protestants from North America. We hope, however, that what follows will call attention to the need for vision as well as stimulate discussion about it.

Biblical foundation

Discussions of this sort often begin with a familiar list of texts: John 17, Ephesians 2 and 4, 1 Corinthians 12... This approach, however, can lead to the conclusion that the reconciliation of Christians (and our calling to be reconcilers in the world) is one theme among others, lifted up in certain parts of the Bible. We believe, to the contrary, that this is the very heart of the good news, central to the story by which we live from Genesis to Revelation. The broad contours of that story, as we have learned it, go something like this.

In the beginning, however it happened, God created the heavens and the earth, a creation of wondrous variety and complexity. And God created it good – that is, full of abundance and harmony (the Hebrew word is *shalom*). At some point in this process of creation, God also created human beings. As a species, we are marked by great natural diversity (e.g., of race and sex and physical ability), but all of us bear, in some mysterious way, the image of God. We are charged to love the Creator, to keep and enjoy the creation, and to live in relationship with one another. Indeed, from the beginning, it is clear that we cannot be who we are created to be apart from one another.

But we don't like to serve anyone, even God. And so, daily, we try to deny our relation to God, to make ourselves into gods who are the measure of all things. In the same way, we deny our relation to other bearers of God's image. In fact, a key part of our sinfulness is a fear of others; or, since the pathology is deeper than that, a fear of otherness. And, as a result, we corrupt God's world, despoil its goodness. Oppression and fragmentation are two of the most prominent signs of our rebellion.

But, amazingly, God will not have done with us. God sets out to show humanity the way it should live by calling a people to be a community of righteousness, a community that lives in conscious covenantal relationship to God. A man named Abraham hears this call and, through all the ups and downs of actual life in the ancient Middle East, God guides the descendants of Abraham and Sarah towards abundant life in the land of Israel – delivering them from slavery, giving them the law, raising up leaders such as Moses and Deborah and David. The people of Israel come to understand that God loves them in a particular way; but, from time to time, prophets in their midst remind them that God, the universal Creator, also loves their neighbours – in a particular way. It is God's purpose, say these prophets, to draw all nations to the holy mountain, that all peoples may live in shalom under God.

But the people of Israel, like all of us, will have none of it. They are rebellious and proud and repeatedly forget the One who has made them. They rely on their own schemes for security and power. And, of course, these are unsubstantial. Israel's national life is destroyed by the Assyrians and the Babylonians and many of the people are taken into exile. But even in the midst of ruins, the prophets cling to God's promises, proclaiming that God will yet make out of Israel's remnant a new community marked by justice for all.

The centuries wait in hope for such fulfilment. And then (most unexpected) there is born in a Bethlehem stable, the most humble of beginnings, a descendant of Ruth and David named Jesus who is, we confess, the Christ – the anointed One, the Messiah, the Son of God. What amazingly good news! Not that we can draw nearer to God, but that God has drawn nearer to us, to the point of sharing our humanity.

In Jesus the Christ we see revealed the gracious, unmerited love of God – a love that comes not because we are loveable but because we are God's children. In him the standards of the world are stood on their head for, says Jesus, in the reign of God the last shall be first. In him, lepers, the poor, women, foreigners, enemies – all those whom society expels to its margins – are shown to be of infinite worth to God. In him, the covenant is extended even to us, for he is the cornerstone of a new household marked by righteousness and peace and wholeness for all people.

But we will have none of that either. And so, on the awful cross of Calvary, we try once again to do away with God's promise and purpose – and then to bury God's child in a tomb. But on the third day God raises him from the dead and triumphs over all our attempts to defeat Christ's lordship. Jesus Christ is raised triumphant over our fear, our pride, our attempts to be our own gods, over the death we seem so determined to embrace. He is raised in the power of God who offers us forgiveness that we might have life in all its relatedness and abundance.

In Christ, the final rule, the reign of God on earth has begun – though we continue to long for its fulfilment in our lives and in the life of the world. By trusting in the God who was in Christ, we find that we do become new creations, free to live no longer for ourselves but for him who died for us. The power of God's Holy Spirit also calls into being a community of those who would be Christ's disciples. This community, the church, is a people defined not by national boundaries or common language or common ethnic identity, but by the shared experience of grace. It is to be a community of such interdependent diversity that the apostle Paul speaks of it as being like a body whose parts, while different, can never say "I have no need of you".

This community gathers in thankful praise around signs of God's empowering spirit, including baptism, the Lord's supper, and a ministry to servanthood. We, its members, are called to be ambassadors of the reconciliation we have experienced in Jesus Christ, witnesses throughout the earth to God's intended wholeness for all creation. We are to show by the way we live, loving God with all our strength and our neighbours as ourselves, the power of God to unite even Jews and Gentiles. In short, the church, though not an end in itself, is called to be nothing less than a visible embodiment of the good news – a sign of God's power to free and unite those who are oppressed and estranged.

Of course, this is not the way we actually live much of the time. But it is the vision of the church's essential nature towards which we live and, thus, is the measure by which our common life is judged. It is a way of recalling that shared life is the norm, and division the problem that demands explanation. The church, in this sense, is always a pilgrim people, living not only by memory but in anticipation of that day when every tear is wiped away and even lions and lambs dwell together.

Christians tell this story in a great variety of ways. Episcopalians (Anglicans) have a special gift for praying it. The Lutheran and Reformed confessions tend "to confess" it, and the Roman Catholic Church makes it teachable through doctrines. Methodists are particularly good at singing it. The Orthodox enact it in the liturgy, while churches such as the Brethren and the Friends stress the importance of embodying it in daily living.

Throughout this century, the ecumenical movement has been saying that when Christians tell this story we generally put too little emphasis on the *whole* church bearing witness to the *whole* gospel in the *whole* world. And that the proper response when we think something is missing from the way others tell it is (except in extreme cases) not division but dialogue, not rejection but renewal. Like all human movements, the ecumenical movement can become preoccupied with its own meetings and structures. But at its root, ecumenism is a call for the one body of Christ to be what it is and to live ever more fully the story it has received from the prophets and apostles.

Theological vision

Perhaps it will help to make all of this more concrete, and to relate it more directly to councils of churches, if we identify three things (rooted in scripture) that, as we see it, make up the core of the ecumenical vision.

1. The ecumenical vision rests on the conviction that Christians (those who confess Jesus Christ as their Lord and Saviour) "are related to one another thanks to actions of God in Jesus Christ which are prior to any decisions they may make". The message from the WCC's first assembly expressed this point in words reminiscent of the apostle Paul: "Christ has made us his own, and he is not divided."

In the United States, our particular context, the church is widely understood to be a voluntary society of those who choose to join it – which means that we can shape it any way we please. But behind the ecumenical movement is the conviction that the church is *God's* and *God's church is one*. This oneness, as presented in the New Testament, is not a self-evident or easy unity. It is the reconciliation of Jew and Gentile, of those whom the world calls enemies.

It is not a cheap unity: the knowledge that we are to welcome one another as Christ has welcomed us calls for repentance for our fearful separation. It is not an abstract unity: our relationship to other parts of the body of Christ is so intense that their joys and sufferings are to become our own. It is not a self-centred unity: our reconciled life is to be a sign of God's reconciling purpose for all creation – that the world may believe that Jesus is the Son of God. It is not a popular unity: our common life must pay special attention to those sisters and brothers whom the world calls "least". It is not an optional unity: insofar as we have communion with Christ through the power of the Holy Spirit, we are bound to all his followers, as it were, by blood – not ours, but his.

The church, of course, is also an all-too-earthen vessel, which means that we constantly, sinfully obscure this God-given communion. For that reason, the ecumenical movement usually speaks of unity as both gift and calling. The ecumenical task is to make the church in which we live more like the church that we confess. But even this task is unthinkable apart from the understanding of unity as a gift of the spirit. We particularly like the way that the great ecumenical leader and archbishop of Canterbury, William Temple, once put it: "We could not seek union if we did not already possess unity, for those who have nothing in common do not deplore their estrangement. It is because we *are* one in allegiance to one Lord that we seek and hope for the way of manifesting that unity in our witness to him before the world." This is the bedrock on which councils of churches are founded.

There are participants in the ecumenical movement who contend that unity is synonymous with – or, at least, dependent on – agreement. Unless carefully defined, however, this can quickly become a form of works righteousness – as if *our* agreement on doctrine or social justice or mission or anything else could create the unity of Christ's body! The unity of the church, said the delegates at the second world conference on Faith and Order (Edinburgh 1937), "does not consist in the agreement of our minds or the consent of our wills... We are one because we are all the objects of the love and grace of God..."

Common confession is of great importance; theological differences should not be minimized, let alone ignored. But it is precisely because we recognize our given relatedness that we strive for common confession through the sharing of differences. Ecumenical dialogue, as the members of the Lutheran-Reformed dialogue committee in the United States pointed out, should not be limited to a conditional logic (if... then). Rather, ecumenism (like the gospel) is grounded in a logic of "because... therefore". Not "if we agree, then we will be one in Christ", but "because we are one in Christ, therefore we are called and empowered to seek common mind in those areas where we have disagreed".

There are other participants in ecumenical ventures who put primary emphasis on Christian diversity. The goal of the movement, however, is not so much to unite diversity as to recognize the proper diversity of our given oneness. Perhaps we can underscore this by stressing that "Christian" is the noun which primarily defines all who are in Christ. We are black Christians and white Christians and are, therefore, related at a level deeper than race. We are female Christians and male Christians and are, therefore, related at a level deeper than gender. We are liberal Christians and conservative Christians and are, therefore, related at a level deeper than ideology. We are American Christians and Cuban Christians and are, therefore, related at a level deeper than nationality. In February 1991, the WCC met for its seventh assembly while American bombs rained down on Iraq. One of the delegates to that meeting was the Chaldean Catholic bishop of Baghdad. "These bombs", he told a group of us from the US, "are also falling on you." It was a profound statement of ecclesiology (the doctrine of the church) in ecumenical perspective.

2. The ecumenical vision, as we understand it, also rests on the conviction that unity is essential to the church's renewal – and vice versa. This may seem obvious, but it has not been so in the history of the church. Those who have emphasized the church's unity have often looked with suspicion on renewal movements because they are disruptive. Meanwhile, those who have pressed for the church's renewal have often regarded "unity" as a code word for "monolithic", "authoritarian", "resistant to change". The genius of the modern ecumenical movement is to insist that this is a false opposition – indeed, that unity and renewal properly define one another. Renewal is meaningless if it doesn't enable Christians to live together across the barriers of the past; but unity is dangerous if divorced from the constant pressure to renew our common life through closer identification with Christ.

Another way to approach this is to point out that ecumenism, far from compromising the faith, should be understood as a "spiritual battle for truth" (Visser 't Hooft) – not a war against each other but a common battle against error based on the assumption that the truth of the gospel is greater than the witness of any single church tradition. A key document from the US Consultation on Church Union (a unity conversation involving nine American denominations) observes that "insofar as Christians have been divided from one another, they have suffered by being deprived of each other's gifts, help and correction". Yes, there are limits to the diversity that the church can embrace (racism, for example, is not a legitimate theological position for the church to hold), but these limits are best tested in ecumenical community. We have received different gifts, as Paul understood, in order to contribute to "the common good" of Christ's body (see 1 Cor. 12).

One clear implication of this is that the ecumenical movement can never be content with interchurch cooperation. The ecumenical vision is not that Christians should learn to get along but that we need each other, and are given each other, in order to be the church. Cooperation, if seen as an end in itself, can actually reinforce the status quo ("You're okay, we're okay") and thus undermine the impulse for renewal. This is a constant danger for councils of churches.

3. The ecumenical vision rests as well on the conviction that the unity and renewal of the church are intimately linked to the unity and renewal of the whole human family – indeed, the whole creation. The vision scripture gives us is not only of a single church, in which Jews and Gentiles eat together, but of a world in which "nation does not lift up sword against nation", "justice will roll down like waters", and "mourning and crying and pain will be no more". Ecumenism is not only a unity movement and a renewal movement, but it is also a movement for justice and peace – one which claims that the church participates in God's work of shalom not just by what it says (its evangelism), and by what it does (its service), but by what it is (its life as a reconciled people). The way we live with each other is to be sign of God's intention for the world as a whole. Whenever the ecumenical movement focuses on intra-Christian disputes without attention to the wider context of human need, it becomes irrelevant. But when this

wider context is taken fully into account, we see again why God's mission demands a reconciled church.

The tendency, of course, is to split the agenda. "It seems to many", notes the report the WCC's fourth assembly (Uppsala 1968), "... that the struggle for Christian unity in its present form is irrelevant to the immediate crisis of our times. The church, they say, should seek its unity through solidarity with those forces in modern life, such as the struggle for racial equality, which are drawing [people] more closely together, and should give up its concern with patching up its own internal disputes." But the ecumenical movement, at its best, insists that these matters are not easily or properly separated. Racism is not "simply" a question of human justice: it is a radical denial of the Christian faith and a source of division for the church. Economic systems that exploit the poor are not "simply" a question of mission; they are a counter-testimony to the gospel and to the church which seeks to live by the values of sharing and solidarity. The problem in South Africa, ecumenical leaders in that country often claimed during the years of apartheid, was that many Christians there never learned what it means to be baptized. "As many of you as were baptized into Christ have clothed yourselves with Christ. There is no longer Jew or Greek, there is no longer slave or free, there is no longer male and female; for all of you are one in Christ Jesus" (Gal. 3:27-28). Can there be any better summary of the ecumenical vision of the church?

2. The History of Councils of Churches

The English word "council" can be thoroughly confusing when used in the ecumenical movement. On the one hand, the word can refer to the governing body of a particular denomination or communion (e.g., the Second Vatican Council of the Roman Catholic Church) or to the councils of the ancient – and, at least to some extent, undivided – church which spoke with authority on matters of faith and practice (e.g., the council of Jerusalem described in Acts 15 or the council of Nicea). On the other hand, the term is also used in reference to the associations or fellowships of still divided churches discussed in this book. Many European languages actually have one word for the first kind of council – *concile* (French), *Konzil* (German), *concilio* (Spanish), *concilium* (Latin) – and another word for the second – *conseil, Rat, consejo, consilium*. In French, for example, the World Council of Churches is called the Conseil œcuménique des Eglises.

The councils we are describing do not make decisions that are binding on their members. "Any authority the Council will have", said William Temple during the formation of the WCC, "consists in the weight which it carries with the churches by its own wisdom." Such councils are marked by what one conference called a "provisional fellowship" which reflects both the unity and division of their members. They are rooted in the oneness we are given; they express the fellowship we now have; and they anticipate the greater unity we seek. As Temple put it: "We may not pretend that the existing unity among Christians is greater than in fact it is; but we should act upon it so far as it is already a reality."

The idea for such a council was unthinkable as long as it was assumed that the Christians of a given place should all belong to one church body, with dissidents the object of exclusion or persecution. By the beginning of the 19th century, however, notions of religious liberty and the separation of church and state had led, particularly in the United States, to a "denominational system" in which various churches lived alongside one another, usually in a state of isolating competition. Organizations were obviously needed to shape public opinion along Christian lines (e.g., the Connecticut

Moral Society, 1813) or to carry out certain projects that were beyond the means of any one denomination (e.g., the American Bible Society, 1816; the American Temperance Society, 1826). These were bodies made up of interested individual Christians, a pattern followed in England with the founding of the YMCA in 1844 and the YWCA eleven years later.

The magnitude and difficulty of world mission, felt ever more intensely during the last half of the 19th century, spurred these developments. The desire to substitute cooperation for competition in overseas mission led to the establishment of "missionary councils" both in Europe (e.g., the German Missionary Council, 1885, and the British Missionary Society, 1912) and in the mission fields of Asia and Africa (e.g., the National Missionary Council of India, Burma and Ceylon, 1912). As their name implies, these councils were composed primarily of mission agencies and were intended to coordinate action for the spread of the gospel.

The Edinburgh missionary conference of 1910, often called the beginning of modern ecumenism, led to the formation of the International Missionary Council (IMC) and gave considerable impetus to the founding of missionary councils in colonized regions. In 1910 there were two national councils through which limited cooperation was possible. By 1928, the year of the first great meeting of the IMC, there were twenty-three.

This same period also saw important changes in the self-understanding and terminology of such councils. India is a good example. In 1922, the National Missionary Council became the National Christian Council of India, Burma and Ceylon, a designation that reflected the increased role played by Asian Christians. The new national council was made up of delegates from regional organizations (though later there was direct representation for some of the larger churches and mission societies), with the express stipulation that at least half of the members must be nationals. The new council also began to expand its range of activities to include such things as famine relief, agricultural education, literature promotion and youth work – though evangelism remained its primary purpose.

The framework for international contact between national Christian councils of this sort was the IMC. By 1948, the year of the WCC's founding assembly, the IMC had thirty member bodies and was in contact with twenty-two other ecumenical organizations in different parts of the world.

Behind this recital of historical fact are the lives of countless men and women whose commitment to cooperative service and witness set the stage for the councils of churches we now know. The leading figure in the early conciliar movement was surely John R. Mott, whose leadership in the IMC enabled him to help form more than twenty-five national Christian councils. For example, from October 1912 to May 1913, Mott held a series of regional and national conferences in India, China, Korea, Japan and Southeast Asia – all leading to greater local cooperation among Christians. "In an unusual degree," writes Kenneth Scott Latourette,

> [Mott] combined a dignified, commanding presence, deep religious faith, evangelistic zeal, the capacity to discern ability and promise in youth and to inspire it, wide-ranging vision, courage, tact, administrative ability, power over public assemblies as a presiding officer, and compelling, convincing speech. A Methodist, a layman, not theologically trained, not using for conversation or public address any other language than his native English, he won the respect and cooperation of thousands of men and women of many races, nations, tongues and ecclesiastical connections.

The development of missionary councils, however, does not tell the whole story. The first national council in which churches were constituent members appears to have been the Protestant Federation of France (1905), a loose association created to enable mutual consultation and to carry out common tasks. This was followed in 1908 by the Federal Council of the Churches of Christ in America, which by 1910 included thirty-one denominations representing the majority of US Protestants. These organizations reflected a growing sense that the voluntary principle was inadequate: the *churches* needed to be together in council. But the emphasis was still on cooperative programming, not growth in unity.

By the middle of the century, however, a new understanding was beginning to emerge – along with new terminology. In 1950, for example, the Federal Council was reborn as the National Council of the Churches of Christ in the USA. In India, the Christian Council became the National Council of Churches in 1956, its constitution specifying that "only organized church bodies are entitled to direct representation in the Council" – a pattern repeated in other parts of the world.

There were two primary reasons for these changes. (1) National independence in places such as India contributed to the indigenization of the churches and to the realization that the membership of foreign mission agencies in national Christian councils undermined the relationship of these bodies to the national community and obscured their true purpose, now increasingly understood as the promotion of Christian fellowship in each place. (2) The birth of the World Council of Churches deeply affected ecumenical organizations around the world. The WCC, inaugurated in 1948, is defined in its Basis as a "fellowship of churches" whose first purpose is "to call the churches to the goal of visible unity". Councils, that is to say, are not simply instruments for cooperative service and evangelism but fellowships through which the churches seek to grow in deeper unity with one another.

The key figure in the early years of the WCC, and the primary architect of its self-understanding, was Willem Visser 't Hooft, general secretary of the World Council from its birth until his retirement in 1966. Without Visser 't Hooft's combination of gifts, wrote one colleague at the time of his death, the WCC might never have existed. "No other person in the leadership of those days possessed the acumen, imagination, statesmanship, experience, daring, energy and languages necessary to bring it into being." Visser 't Hooft wrote in his *Memoirs:*

The worst thing that could happen to the Council would be that it should come to be considered as just another cog in the ecclesiastical machine. My role was not to invent brand-new ideas, but to discover the most forward-looking initiatives in the life of the churches and to seek to make them fruitful for the whole ecumenical family.

The first regional council of churches was the East Asia Christian Conference (now called the Christian Conference of Asia), which held its inaugural assembly in 1959. At present, there are regional councils in Africa, the Pacific, Europe, the Middle East, the Caribbean and Latin America, in addition to Asia.

No one knows the number of local councils of churches, but the *Dictionary of the Ecumenical Movement* suggests that worldwide they must number in the tens of thousands. A recent study of local ecumenism in the United States found that local and state councils tend to be "pragmatic", focused on "doing together what cannot be done at all or as effectively alone". Cooperative service and legislative advocacy dominate their agendas, though concern for questions of Faith and Order is by no means absent.

Three recent developments need to be named in any history of councils of churches.

1. Since the Second Vatican Council, the Roman Catholic Church has become a member of more than forty national councils, as well as many local and regional bodies. The Roman Catholic Church is not a member of the WCC, though it works closely with the Council, especially through what is known as the Joint Working Group.

2. Churches in several countries are exploring new models of conciliar life. What is sometimes called the "churches together" model (now being tried in the United Kingdom, Australia, New Zealand and Canada) attempts to avoid the notion that a council is a structure alongside of, or even over and against, the churches. "The council" will not act unless there is a consensus among the member churches to do so, and church leaders play a prominent role in any decision-making. Other councils (e.g., the Middle East Council of

Churches and the Christian Council of Sweden) have structured themselves according to "families of churches":
Roman Catholic, Orthodox and Protestant. This model
allows for representation that is not solely based on the size
and resources of individual churches.

3. A good deal of attention has been paid over the past
generation to the theological self-understanding of councils
of churches. It is this discussion that we will explore in the
next chapter.

3. The Theological Basis of Councils of Churches

We have already noted that councils of churches are a new thing in the church. Prior to the modern ecumenical movement, Christians formed organizations dedicated to particular tasks. Contemporary councils often have roots in these significant movements and federations. But when *churches* commit themselves to one another for common service, witness, worship, study and dialogue, something new is happening – something that is beyond the isolating divisions of the past though not yet the full, visible communion that appears indistinctly before us. Conciliarity, writes the Orthodox theologian Nikos Nissiotis, "is a quite new phenomenon and we have at our disposal no appropriate ecclesiological terms to describe it. We here have to face a reality that goes beyond our capacity to conceptualize it theologically."

In the past fifty years Christians have witnessed several attempts to fill this theological void. The most significant document on the theology of councils of churches is the so-called Toronto statement, drafted by the World Council's central committee in 1950. All of the other texts to which we will refer in this chapter are, in a sense, commentaries on this attempt to define the meaning of membership in the WCC. The debate was taken up again by the fourth world conference on Faith and Order in 1963, the same year that the national council in the United States produced an important working paper on "The Ecclesiological Significance of Councils of Churches". Since that time, the WCC has sponsored three international consultations for national and regional councils and, in recent years, has reflected extensively on its own meaning and purpose through a study process called "Towards a Common Understanding and Vision of the World Council of Churches" (CUV). Other councils have followed suit. In the United States, for example, the National Council of the Churches of Christ (NCCC) authorized an ecclesiology study task force to report on "the ecclesiological meaning of membership in the NCCC" and to provide "new insights concerning ecumenical life in the American churches today".

In this chapter, we will attempt to summarize this half-century of discussion by making four points. These theological affirmations are not our own; but the way we present them is intended to be prescriptive as well as descriptive. We believe that serious attention to these four points can strengthen the life and witness of most councils of churches.

Fellowship

A council, to quote from the Basis of the WCC, is best understood as a *"fellowship of churches"*. The use of the term fellowship (a translation of the Greek word *koinonia)* means that the WCC is seen as "more than a mere functional association of churches set up to organize activities in areas of common interest" (CUV). The essence of the council, to put it another way, is not only what the churches *do* together, but also what they *are* together.

Not all councils of churches employ the language of fellowship in their definitional statements, but this point is in our experience widely endorsed by those who give leadership to these bodies, at whatever level. A fellowship, they often attest, is not something *we* can create. The use of the term reminds us that thanks to what God has done, our churches are not strangers to one another, whatever their historical separations. Councils of churches are partial, provisional expressions of the fellowship that is commonly ours in Jesus Christ.

From this there follows an important implication. The essence of a council of churches is the relationship of the member churches to one another, not their relationship to the structure of the council. The CUV text puts it this way with reference to the WCC: "The Council *is* the fellowship of the churches on the way towards full *koinonia.* It *has* a structure and organization in order to serve as an instrument for the churches as they work towards *koinonia* in faith, life and witness; but the WCC is not to be identified with this structure..."

There are countless organizations that provide services on behalf of churches. These should not be confused, however, with a council – a fellowship – of the churches themselves.

Whenever churches see a council as "them" rather than "us" (as "that organization" rather than "our fellowship"), then conciliar life has been radically misunderstood. Without a recognition of this point, churches tend to avoid the accountability that ought to go with membership in a council of churches. The NCCC's ecclesiology study report underscores this:

> Repeatedly it is said that the NCCC needs to be transformed. Of course, every ecumenical body needs periodically to be renewed; no conciliar structure should be thought of as a permanent part of the ecclesial landscape since its animating vision must be of ever-deeper communion. However, if the ecumenical witness of the NCCC is not what it ought to be, then it is not just "the council" that needs to be transformed but the *churches*. The council can be restructured without ever touching the fundamental ecclesiological question of our *churches'* relationship to one another...

A council's structure may need reform, even drastic change; but the basic question is always whether the ecumenical commitment of the member churches, their willingness to grow in deeper fellowship with one another, is adequate to the imperatives of the gospel.

We have been talking about how churches, through their leaders and other representatives, often think of councils as bodies apart from themselves. It is also true, however, that the staff or assembly of a council structure may act and speak as if the council were something alongside of, even over against, the churches. A council, ecumenical leaders often insist, should be an instrument not only of the churches but of the ecumenical movement. It should be "a thorn in the flesh of the churches" (Lukas Vischer), prodding them to go beyond what they initially see as their agenda. This surely is true. The point we are making, however, is that the work of "the council" will likely be dismissed or resisted unless the churches recognize that the challenge (the thorn) comes from their mutual commitment to one another, not from some group of professional ecumenists. One purpose of the staff and structure of a council is to hold the churches accountable to the commitments they have made by virtue of their participation in this fellowship.

All of this suggests criteria for the churches' evaluation of their life together. For example:

- Do the work and structure of the council serve to build up fellowship among the member churches?
- Does the structure enable them to know one another better? Does it provide space for continual conversation about the nature of this fellowship and the impact it has on the churches' particular self-understandings?
- Does the structure reflect the conviction that every member church is an equally valued contributor? (If the council is essentially a fellowship of the churches, then the contribution of each member is not a function of its size or resources but of its being in Christ.)

Marks of membership

Membership in a council of churches does *not* necessarily imply that a church recognizes doctrines and practices of the others or even, in the words of the Toronto statement, "that each church must regard the other member churches as churches in the true and full sense of the word". It is relatively easy to form an association of churches that all conceive of the church in the same basic way. But that is precisely the crucial new fact about councils: they express fellowship among churches that may or may not be able to recognize and accept each other fully. Councils of churches exist in order that *divided* churches may be brought into "living contact" (Toronto statement).

It is not enough, however, to stop with these negatives. While membership in a council of churches need not mean full mutual recognition, it does mean:

- acknowledging that the other member communions, in some sense, belong to Christ ("A council", says the WCC's Faith and Order commission, "depends on the readiness of the churches to recognize each other as confessing the same Christ, though this confession may take radically different forms.");

- affirming that membership in the body of Christ is more inclusive than membership in our own denomination or communion ("It is impossible", wrote the Orthodox theologian Georges Florovsky, one of the authors of the Toronto statement, "to state or discern the true limits of the church simply by canonical signs or marks." The boundaries of the church are determined by the presence of the Holy Spirit, and this does not always coincide with our definitions.);
- recognizing in the other members crucial elements of the one church (e.g., proclamation of the gospel teaching based on scripture, mission in the name of Jesus Christ, worship of the triune God, and celebration of the sacraments instituted by our Lord).

If a church does not recognize these things in the other members, then its participation will, indeed, be superficial. It will see the council as a purely utilitarian structure rather than an expression of fellowship given in Christ – however partial and preliminary. (The CUV document notes, by the way, that membership in the WCC "does not oblige churches to understand the phrase [fellowship of churches] in a particular way", but "it does commit them to dialogue about this").

Beyond all this, membership in a council, if taken seriously, should signal an awareness of our own deficiency. The Toronto statement spoke of this as a "holy dissatisfaction", a recognition that insofar as Christians live apart from one another we are impoverished. This means that each church should be regarded as a receiver as well as a contributor to the fellowship of the council. The widely respected Roman Catholic ecumenist Jean-Marie Tillard makes this point directly: "Convinced that she possesses what is required for ecclesial fullness, [the Roman Catholic Church] does not pretend to possess all of it as perfectly as she should. In councils of churches, she too has much to receive."

None of this, of course, excludes "extremely frank speaking to each other" (Toronto statement). Indeed, the bonds implied in membership ought to allow, even encourage, such speaking. Councils of churches are arenas in which "mutual affirmation and admonition" can take place – as long as it is done in order to build up the body of Christ.

In developing its statement "Towards a Common Understanding and Vision", the WCC identified nine marks of membership. We list them here as a possible reference point for other councils:

- To be a member means nuturing the ability to pray, live, act and grow together in community – sometimes through struggle and conflict – with churches from differing backgrounds and traditions. It implies the willingness and capacity to deal with disagreement through theological discussion, prayer and dialogue, treating contentious issues as matters for common theological discernment rather than political victory.

- To be a member means helping one another to be faithful to the gospel, and questioning one another if any member is perceived to move away from the fundamentals of the faith or obedience to the gospel. The integrity of the fellowship is preserved through the exercise of responsibility for one another in the spirit of common faithfulness to the gospel, rather than by judgment and exclusion.

- To be a member means participating in ministries that extend beyond the boundaries and possibilities of any single church and being ready to link one's own specific local context with the global reality and to allow that global reality to have an impact in one's local situation.

- To be a member means being part of a fellowship that has a voice of its own. While the churches are free to choose whether or not to identify themselves with the voice of the WCC when it speaks, they are committed to giving serious consideration to what the Council says or does on behalf of the fellowship as a whole.

- To be a member means making a commitment to seek to implement within the life and witness of one's own church the agreements reached through joint theological study and reflection by the total fellowship.

- To be a member means participating in a fellowship of sharing and solidarity, supporting other members in their needs and struggles, celebrating with them their joys and hopes.

- To be a member means understanding the mission of the church as a joint responsibility shared with others, rather than engaging in missionary or evangelistic activities in isolation from each other, much less in competition with or proselytism of other Christian believers.
- To be a member means entering into a fellowship of worship and prayer with the other churches, nurturing concrete opportunities for shared worship and prayer while respecting the limitations imposed by specific traditions.
- To be a member means taking a full part in the life and work of the WCC and its activities, including praying for the Council and all its member churches, being represented at assemblies, making regular financial contributions to its work according to one's possibilities and sharing the WCC's concerns with local parishes, congregations and worshipping communities.

Deeper ecumenical commitment

The fellowship that is at the heart of a council of churches is not "something abstract and static" but "a dynamic, relational reality" (CUV) which ought to change and, hopefully, deepen as a result of common membership in the council. The Toronto statement says that "... no church is obliged to change its ecclesiology as a *consequence* of membership in the World Council". But, argues the great ecumenical leader, Lesslie Newbigin, it would have been better to say that "no church is obliged to change as a *condition* of membership in the Council". Membership does not mean that churches enter the fellowship of a council agreeing about the nature of the church. To stop there, however, is to reduce the council to a debating society and implicitly endorse the present form of conciliar relationship as an adequate expression of Christian fellowship. "It is good", writes Newbigin, "that churches should be reassured in respect to any fear that they might surrender their convictions for the sake of some [hu]man-made organization. But it is also good that they should be reminded that they might fall into the hands of the Living God" – and be changed.

To put it another way, the fellowship experienced in conciliar ecumenism is not only rooted in what the churches are but in what they are called to become. Through their mutual engagement in a council, the churches should expect (should demand!) to be challenged to deeper and more costly ecumenical commitment – by the staff and, more importantly, by each other. If this is not the case, then our very success at fostering cooperation institutionalizes our present separations.

When the Toronto statement was written in 1950, the churches were able to affirm that membership in the WCC meant a willingness "to consult together... recognize their solidarity with each other, render assistance to each other in case of need, and refrain from such actions as are incompatible with brotherly [and sisterly] relationships". The marks of membership included in the CUV text (and listed above) would, if approved, signal considerable growth in fellowship over the past fifty years.

Instruments of unity

It follows from what we have said that councils of churches must see themselves as provisional, must always be prepared to die in order that fuller manifestations of communion may be born. They are steps towards deeper fellowship *as the church*, which is why councils dare not become service organizations aimed at self-perpetuation. Councils, through their programmes and decision-making bodies, must always insist on the growing commitment of the member churches to each other. Otherwise, they can actually hinder the work of ecumenism. The WCC's Faith and Order commission puts this issue in the form of questions:

> Do councils continue to serve the cause of unity, or do they rather institutionalize a limited degree of unity and perpetuate division? Do they serve to go on to the next step on the road, or do they give the churches a good conscience by leaving them at a stage where they are not quite divided but not yet united?

26

Tillard uses a more graphic analogy. Unless the aim is visible unity, he writes, councils run the risk of becoming like De Gaulle's description of the Vichy government: an institution whose sole result is "to make the shame of defeat acceptable".

Churches are often all too ready to leave ecumenism to "the council" – as if conciliar membership means that they have hired persons to be ecumenical for them! When this happens, councils lose their significance as instruments of the ecumenical movement.

We want to stress that decisions about unity are properly left to the churches; but councils are a place where trust can grow, where divisive issues can be discussed, where reception of the results of ecumenical dialogues can be encouraged. What we call councils of churches, said Lukas Vischer at the 1971 international consultation, are the structural expressions of the churches' ecumenical commitment. As such, "they constitute the setting, created by the churches themselves, within which the promise of renewal may be heard..." They are, thus, "instruments of unity" (1971 consultation), even "preliminary expressions" of unity (Vancouver assembly, 1983) – but not the full *koinonia* that is Christ's gift and calling.

If we were to write a "basis" statement for a council, drawing on the points made in this chapter, it might look something like this:

The _____ Council of Churches is a fellowship of churches which, in response to the gospel as revealed in scripture, confess Jesus Christ as Saviour and Lord. Relying upon the power of the Holy Spirit, these churches covenant with one another to engage in common mission and to manifest ever more fully the unity of the church.

In affirming this covenant, our churches confess that apart from one another we are impoverished and repent of our frequent failure to make our own the joys and struggles of the other member communions. We recognize that membership in the Council entails the responsibility of bearing witness to the gospel as we have received it, but also the opportunity of being challenged and inspired by perspectives other than our own. We acknowledge that the Council is a forum in which dialogue about the nature and purpose of the church rightly takes place, a forum in which all members are responsible for speaking and hearing the truth in love. We also acknowledge that, while membership in the _____ does not necessarily imply full recognition of the other members as "church", it is based on the recognition of certain sacred bonds between us, including:

–   proclamation through word and deed of the gospel, God's reconciling and redeeming love for all creation as revealed in Christ and recorded in scripture;
–   incorporation into Christ through baptism [if all of the members practise baptism];
–   worship through word and sacrament of the one God, Father, Son and Holy Spirit;
    ministries of service and witness in Christ's name.

These are significant signs of the oneness we already have as followers of Jesus Christ. We also recognize, however, that our life together as a council of churches, if it is led by the Spirit, can never be static. We pray that our relationships may deepen and expand towards the day when all Christians in this place visibly love one another, and all of God's children, even as Christ has loved us.

4. Membership in Councils of Churches

Most councils of churches have a theological basis, however minimal, which in effect determines the range of membership and defines what holds the fellowship together.* A model for many other councils is the Basis of the WCC: "The World Council of Churches is a fellowship of churches which confess the Lord Jesus Christ as God and Saviour according to the scriptures and therefore seek to fulfill together their common calling to the glory of the one God, Father, Son and Holy Spirit."

When the WCC's Constitution was first adopted, it read: "The World Council of Churches is a fellowship of churches which accept our Lord Jesus Christ as God and Saviour" – a formulation that echoed the Basis of the YMCA (drafted in 1855) and, before that, Titus 2:13. In his "Explanatory Memorandum", sent to the churches along with the proposed Constitution, William Temple argued that "the Basis is an affirmation of the faith of the participating churches and not a credal test to judge persons or churches. It is an affirmation of the incarnation and the atonement." At the WCC's third assembly in 1961, the basis was expanded to include reference to the authority of scripture and to set the Christological confession ("the Lord Jesus Christ as God and Saviour") within a trinitarian framework ("to the glory of the one God, Father, Son and Holy Spirit").

These changes, as Visser 't Hooft pointed out in his *Memoirs,* had important repercussions:

> It helped give the Eastern Orthodox churches greater confidence in the World Council and to bring in the many Orthodox churches which had not yet become members. It reassured the more "evangelical" elements in the constituency of the International Missionary Council who had hesitated about the integration with the World Council.

But, despite Temple's claim to the contrary, the Basis also has the effect of excluding certain communities, e.g., many

---

* The focus of this chapter is on the range and conditions of membership. The expectations that go with membership in a council of churches have already been discussed in ch. 3.

Unitarians (who cannot make the trinitarian confession) and the Mormons (who have a source of revealed, written authority in addition to the scriptures). The boundaries on membership for any council are determined by its core confession.

The Orthodox churches

In the early years of the conciliar movement (i.e., prior to the formation of the WCC), the churches involved were primarily what we now call mainline Protestant. Several Orthodox churches, however, were charter members of the World Council, and all of the Eastern and Oriental Orthodox churches had joined by the early 1960s. Orthodox communities are now active participants in local and national councils around the world. "It must be stressed", said the participants in one international gathering of Orthodox leaders,

> that the participation of the Orthodox in the ecumenical movement of today is not, in principle, a revolution in the history of Orthodoxy, but is a natural consequence of the constant prayer of the church "for the union of all". It constitutes another attempt, like those made in the patristic period, to apply the apostolic faith to new historical situations and existential demands. What is in a sense new today is the fact that this attempt is being made together with other Christian bodies with whom there is no full unity.

In recent years, Orthodox church representatives have also expressed a series of concerns that all councils would do well to take seriously:
- Within the life of a council, issues "alien to the Orthodox tradition and ethos" (e.g., the ordination of women and the place of homosexuals in the church) may be given programmatic attention.
- The structures and procedures of conciliar life often seem at odds with the Orthodox ecclesiological self-understanding. A structure in which every small Protestant church gets a vote and the majority of votes wins is decidedly foreign to Orthodox sensibilities. The differences, however, run deeper. Western Protestants tend to see the ecumenical problem in terms of needing to unite

fragmented denominations, each of which witnesses in important but partial ways to the gospel. The Orthodox generally dismiss this approach as "interconfessional adjustment". For them, the ecumenical problem is schism, the rejection of orthodox faith and order by other Christians.
– The Orthodox strongly object to what is perceived as proselytism in historic The Orthodox lands. How, they ask, can churches be members with us in the fellowship of a council and, at the same time, send missionaries to the former Eastern bloc without apparent regard for indigenous Orthodox communities?

The Roman Catholic Church

The Roman Catholic Church began to participate in ecumenical councils of churches following the dramatic changes associated with Vatican II. The Catholic church decided not to become a member of the WCC in the early 1970s, but it is now a member of nearly sixty national councils, and three regional councils (Pacific, Middle East, Caribbean).

The 1993 *Directory for the Application of Principles and Norms on Ecumenism,* issued by the Pontifical Council for Promoting Christian Unity, welcomes this growing involvement and offers guidelines for conciliar participation:
– Decision regarding membership is the responsibility of bishops in the areas served by the council. For national councils, this is the episcopal conference in that country, except where the country has only a single diocese.
– "Clear and precise agreement" on the council's system of representation and voting rights, its decision-making processes, its manner of making public statements, and the authority attributed to such statements needs to be reached before membership is taken up.
– The Catholic church should be represented by "well-qualified and committed persons" who understand the limits beyond which they cannot commit the church without referring a matter under discussion to the bishops who oversee their participation.

– If a council is to have Roman Catholic membership, it must take full account of these specifications.

Pentecostal and evangelical churches

Contrary to popular belief, Pentecostal and evangelical churches are members of some councils. Several Pentecostal and "Pentecostal-like" African Instituted Churches are members, for example, of the World Council. For the most part, however, such churches have avoided conciliar participation based on a general mistrust of the ecumenical movement and a more specific fear that council membership would associate them with statements and actions that are too politically and theologically liberal. It is also true that conciliar churches have often failed to welcome Pentecostals and evangelicals out of a fear that their participation would compromise existing ecumenical priorities. As former WCC staff member Marlin VanElderen pointed out, there is a constant tension within councils "between *comprehensiveness* – a desire to include the broadest possible spectrum of Christian groups and churches – and *focus* – a desire to foster a clear vision of what ecumenism requires and to live out that vision in common undertakings".

The search for a wider involvement

The need to expand involvement beyond the traditional circle of churches is, however, a major theme in recent ecumenical documents. The report of the ecclesiology study task force of the National Council of the Churches of Christ (USA) is a case in point:

> From their varied perspectives, the pioneers of the modern ecumenical movement reached out to initiate engagement with the widest range of Christian diversity they could then imagine, even accepting the painful acknowledgment that all participants might not accept each other as true Christian churches... We need to return to such basics, to seek to gather as the most comprehensive possible assembly of Christian communions and to renew the journey together towards the fullness of one body in Christ. If ecumenical dialogue is to prefigure in some small way

that feast of full unity, it must engage the entire breadth of actual Christian communities. That means that the deepest and most intractable divisions should be manifest in that dialogue, which must include as many voices as possible.

With that in mind, the task force called for the creation of a "new and larger forum" where members of the NCC could meet with Roman Catholics, Pentecostals and evangelicals without raising the question of membership in the council, at least initially. A similar idea has been proposed by the WCC's general secretary, Konrad Raiser, and was commended for further study by the World Council's 1998 assembly in Harare.

In the context where we work, the United States, the most extensive and difficult discussion regarding membership in recent years has revolved around the Universal Fellowship of Metropolitan Community Churches, a denomination explicitly founded to minister to those persons alienated from Christian community because of their sexual orientation. The question of whether the UFMCC should be admitted as a member, or even as an official observer, has strained the bonds of fellowship within the NCC. Admission of the UFMCC would surely be interpreted by the media, and by many Christians, as a formal legitimation of homosexuality; and this would likely undermine the capacity of the NCC to promote common witness among its other members. Rejection is also problematic, however, for a body that presently includes churches holding widely differing views on such matters as the nature of the church, the meaning of the sacraments, the acceptability of abortion, and the role of women in church leadership. One participant in NCC activities puts the issue this way: "Is membership in the NCC determined by confession of faith in Jesus Christ and the affirmation of the gospel, or is there another principle at work which is more determinative?" This is a question that all councils must face when considering membership applications.

5. The Relationship between Theory and Practice

When a new board member was called by a council director to debrief after his first meeting, he said: "It seemed like we hopped from issue to issue. Tell me what the one or two main priorities of this council are. Help me to get a handle on all this."

After the director responded with a basic statement of purpose, she then went on to specify the "marks of a truly ecumenical body":[1] shared worship, dialogue, ecumenical advocacy, evangelism, social mission and cooperation.

It was clear from his reaction, however, that the council had been doing an inadequate job of making those connections. The new board member had a good suggestion. "Why don't you organize the agenda under those categories, to remind us all of what we are doing and why we are doing it?" The idea made sense, and the director wondered why she hadn't thought of it before.

These marks of a truly ecumenical body connect theory to practice. Although councils are not churches, their existence is rooted in what it means to be the church, and thus what it means to be churches together through a council. It stands to reason that, because councils of churches have no authentic existence apart from their members, they should be shaped by certain ideas about the nature and mission of the church. When they meet together, they have a "churchly" quality.

These ideas should, and often do, affect the ways member churches live out their lives together through a council. For example, as *Baptism, Eucharist and Ministry* affirms, the church's ministry is rooted in "the calling of the whole people of God".[2] This concept of catholicity has affected the make-up of councils of churches. Whether or not councils encompass all churches of Christ as formal members, they often cast a wide net in their operations. Through deliberating, living and working together, the churches are given opportunities to discern more clearly their own gifts and the gifts of others, and to use those gifts for the good of the whole. And through the diversity of persons participating in the council, the "whole people of God" representatively is involved in ecumenical ministry.

In addition, just as worship is a central focus of a church's life, so it should be a significant aspect of the churches' life together. Furthermore, when the churches come together they have a *special calling to pray for unity.* Despite all the difficulties ecumenical worship continues to pose, we still make the effort because it roots us in our common calling, binds us to each other, and reminds us of why we have come together.

Common service also is a key element of conciliar work because, as the churches affirmed in the Toronto statement, they are called to be in service to each other and to their neighbours.

Through diaconal sharing of experience, personnel, resources and support, the churches already show a sign of the unity given to us by God. By concrete signs of caring together – often done more efficiently and effectively in common – we already manifest our oneness in the body of Christ.

Councils of churches also cannot avoid making some confessional statement, no matter how minimal, as the constitutional basis on which the churches can come together. When they become members, they do so by acknowledging that they adhere to some common formula – for example, that "Jesus Christ is Lord and Saviour". In addition, whenever the churches speak together through the council – by highlighting issues that need attention, or by suggesting ways to address them, or by defining and clarifying the nature of a problem – they also exercise a witnessing function.

Finally, the quest for justice, which is at the heart of the gospel, shapes the practice of councils of churches. In a variety of ways, the churches together point beyond themselves to the eschatological vision of shalom.

Examples of the ways councils live out these marks are as diverse as the councils themselves. They are shaped by their context – urban, suburban, rural; state, regional, local; which churches have joined and which have not; and whether people of other faiths are a sizeable presence in the region. They have different ways of defining membership and making decisions. Some churches ask a designated representative from each member to act on their behalf. Others invite "families of churches" (defined by tradition) to designate representatives, such as the Middle East Council of Churches. Some enable church-related bodies (such as Church Women United, Bible Societies, ecumenical consortia of seminaries) to sit at the conciliar table. And some agree that no actions will be taken unless most, or all, achieve consensus (Council of Churches in Britain and Ireland, Churches Together in England). The following are some illustrations of approaches that are consistent with the marks of a truly ecumenical body. They are ways we can tell the full story together.

Shared worship

Planning and experiencing shared worship often provides the clearest lens through which people experience both the pain of and the possibilities beyond our divisions. Because the scriptures are a source that all Christians hold in common, ecumenical Bible study is a good way for Christians to encounter each other through the text they hold in common. It also is a good way to begin planning an ecumenical worship service.

Christians also can pray together – something we take for granted now, but prior to the 20th century even many Protestants were not praying together. Before Vatican II shared prayer was out of the question for Roman Catholics. This is no longer the case, but in English-speaking countries new obstacles have arisen because of debates about inclusive language. We have not yet arrived at a mutually satisfactory solution to this problem. Compromise probably is the best possible approach – one that will not please purists of any persuasion.

Councils of churches have used a variety of approaches to common prayer. They have invited a member to pray in the words of his or her own tradition. They have invited intercessions from the assembled, and allowed those present to pray out of the concerns of their own hearts and those of their churches. They have used *the* prayer in common to all Christian spiritual traditions – namely, the Lord's prayer. They have prayed the psalms – another aspect of prayer common to all. They have used shared hymnody – a form of prayer. They have drawn directly from biblical texts to form their prayers. And they have developed or used prayers that focus specifically on the longing for Christian unity. The latter are growing in number, thanks to the many ecumenical gatherings for which worship resources have been developed.

These resources also can be a great help to people planning ecumenical worship services. Agreement is building – at least through frequency of use – for certain orders of service that draw on morning and evening prayer familiar to many traditions. These suggested services have been developed by the Consultation on Common Texts, the office for worship of the World Council of Churches, the Consultation on Church Union, the planners of the Week of Prayer for Christian Unity, and others.

Such resources do not eliminate the pain that comes with realizing that many Christians cannot come to the same eucharistic table together. Even this pain, however, can be a teaching moment, helping people understand viscerally the scandal of our divisions and the need to heal them.

Dialogue

Some forms of dialogue are informal, some are structured. Some are occasional, some are ongoing. Dialogue is one means for churches and their members to get to know each other better and understand each other more fully. This process takes time. It grows out of the foundation of developing trust and respect.

This can be through something as simple as two religious leaders driving to a meeting together and talking along the way. It may involve regular gatherings of religious leaders for common Bible study, support, and serious exchange about differences. The discussions can be wide-ranging – everything from a confidential airing of common problems, to a comparison of theory and practice, to the sustained wrestling with a sore source of division.

Because particular people cycle through leadership positions in churches, these tasks never are completed. They must be sustained as an ongoing part of ecumenical life.

Ecumenical advocacy

Such "encouragement" entails holding churches accountable to the commitments they have made, whether by virtue of their membership in a council, or by their own internal ecumenical texts. It involves helping churches see how they can move to the fullness of visible Christian unity. Some forms of ecumenical advocacy seem obvious, but they are not always so to member churches in a council: for example, encouraging the churches to include information about conciliar membership in their own denominational directory; printing information about council membership in their annual report; including stories about ecumenical activities in the church's newspaper, newsletter, bulletin; making their involvements visible at their annual meetings; providing regular reports to church boards of directors; making clear provision for financial obligations in the regular budgeting process of the church.

Churches should hold each other accountable for the promises they have made through their membership. Enough space should be available in their life together so they can ask each other specific and sometimes hard questions about what it means to be in covenantal relationship. Churches also should press their ecumenical staff for a public accounting of ways that staff have helped their members to be accountable – even in face of their reluctance!

Evangelism

Christian witness occurs when the sharer makes the gospel manifest, through word or deed. Because this is an essential aspect of Christian discipleship, it should be a significant aspect of our life together. The task of evangelism poses unique challenges, however, for ecumenically committed churches. How can particular churches sing the Lord's song aloud without diminishing or denigrating the voices of

Christian brothers and sisters? How can they sing that song together?

One council of churches that tried to answer these questions developed the following guidelines:

1. In programmes or services with the stated purpose of Christian witness, care should be taken to *present the gospel without undue emphasis on denominational distinctives.* (Denominational distinctives are a significant part of history, but are distinguishable from what Christians throughout history have regarded as essential to the gospel.)

2. The focus of interdenominational (and denominational) evangelistic endeavours will be to *share the gospel without denigration of denominational distinctives.*

3. Ecumenical accountability in Christian witness will be *sensitive to historic relationships,* choosing normally to reach the unbeliever rather than to awaken and shift the nominal believer. Ecumenical partners recognize, however, that cultural mobility is an inevitable and even appropriate phenomenon in American society and may include movement among denominations.[3]

The roles of councils of churches can be to help their members and other churches in their area understand and embrace certain common guidelines for responsible evangelism. Councils can serve as a sounding board for proposed evangelistic projects. They can provide a table for dialogue when particular concerns arise. They can provide means for common witness – for example, holding an ecumenical training conference about the nature of Christian stewardship; sponsoring shared ecumenical radio or television programming; holding ecumenical worship services open to the public.

Social mission and witness

How churches approach the prophetic aspect of their life together depends on the issue. On some subjects, they will agree completely. On other matters, they may agree on the policy but disagree on the approach that leads them there.

For example, Protestant, Roman Catholic and Orthodox churches often agree on their official opposition to capital punishment in America, but they make their cases on different grounds because they take different approaches to ethical argumentation. On yet other topics, churches disagree vigorously.

When churches agree, they may have different comfort levels on the method, style or strategy they use to advocate their position. Some religious leaders are comfortable working behind the scenes with public officials. Some are accustomed to making their appeals to congregants in open letters, and relying on grassroots response. Others – fewer than in an earlier era – are comfortable in front of a news camera and are willing to be publicly visible.

These variations provide distinct options for the churches in a council. Some councils have developed guidelines to help churches discern suitable approaches depending on the situation. The Joint Working Group between the Roman Catholic Church and the World Council of Churches prepared a helpful paper on this subject: *The Ecumenical Dialogue on Moral Issues: Potential Sources of Common Witness or of Divisions.*[4] All such efforts involve consultation – sometimes lengthy and time-consuming – before the language in a policy can be agreed upon (if possible), and strategies for implementing that policy can be developed.

If churches agree on the conclusion but disagree on how they make their case, sometimes releasing different statements simultaneously is a way to show solidarity and heighten public impact.

When churches clearly disagree, sometimes the most helpful approach a council can take is to provide a forum for structured conversation, and model how civil discourse can occur among deeply divided Christians. When people listen to each other – really listen – they may be able to dispel stereotypes. They may find common ground on peripheral issues related to the divisive core. For example, on an issue as divisive as abortion, religious leaders may find themselves agreeing on changes in public policy that would reduce the need and demand for abortions. On the physician-assisted suicide debate, they may be able to agree on the societal issues driving the discussion.

In addition, those issues on which religious leaders and clergy are willing to spend significant time, in comparison with competing demands, are few in a period of post-downsizing stress syndrome (in the North American context). So approaches have to be realistic and efficient. If a phone call to a couple of key public officials will work almost as well as a meeting, these days one opts for the call.

Strategies that are loose and give a lot of lead time – that provide a variety of ways clergy and congregations can respond, depending on individual circumstances – often work best.

Cooperation

This might seem to be the easiest area for ecumenical effort among churches, but that is not always the case. Sometimes competition dampens the cooperative spirit. Sometimes self-absorption obscures opportunities. Furthermore, if churches get stuck at the level of cooperation, rather than seeing it as a manifestation of our growing life together, they fall short of the fullness of the gospel mandate to unity.

When all these resistances can be overcome, however, the possibilities for cooperation are limited only by one's imagination. Local and regional councils have sponsored shared chaplaincy programmes in a variety of settings: hospitals, nursing homes, prisons, homes for persons with special needs, etc. They have initiated vacation Bible schools. (A council located in an area of new Hispanic-speaking immigrants was able to turn theirs into a multilingual experience, involving Pentecostal and evangelical churches that previously had had no contact with the council.) Councils have fostered food pantries, second-hand shops, cooperative feeding programmes and emergency shelters. They have sponsored emergency fuel programmes, promoted ecumenical activities for youth groups, launched buying cooperatives for office supplies and heating fuel.

State councils have organized disaster relief operations to assist regions hit by floods, hurricanes, snow and ice storms, earthquakes, etc. They have initiated periodic meetings of denominational interest groups: Christian educators, stewardship staff, communications experts, personnel administrators. They have enabled special programmes where common interests are met, such as shared leadership training. Cooperation for mutual support and up-building has been a special strength of regional councils, such as the All Africa Conference of Churches, which has implemented diverse programmes in "the selfhood of the church", refugees and emergency assistance, research and development, and communications training.

Sometimes the possibilities for cooperation can be seen only by someone with an overview of the whole picture, who presents ideas and tests them out. Other times recommendations come from members. Either way, councils can and should use these cooperative ventures to educate participants about the ecumenical mandate, and how their particular venture fits into this quest for wholeness and unity.

These, then, are only a few examples of the many ways that councils of churches can fulfill their mandate. One way to help member churches see the degree to which they are meeting their ecumenical responsibilities would be to provide a survey with specific questions, and let the churches rate themselves. Boards of directors of churches should be encouraged to participate in this process, thus turning the audit into an educational tool as well as a measurable assessment. Churches could be encouraged to set specific goals for the following year, and to continue assessing their progress on an annual basis. Member churches could be recognized for their achievements and encouraged to press on.

Councils of churches can conduct a similar audit. Producing an annual report is an ideal time to step back and assess the degree to which council programmes and projects are consistent with and help further their fundamental aims.

It is tempting to look at all the programmatic means possible for churches to achieve their aim, and miss the message.

Churches in council are not a *thing*. They are a *covenantal relationship*, seeking full visible unity.

Will we hit the mark? Probably not, but unless we know where we are aiming, we will not have any way to check on whether we are headed in the right direction.

NOTES

[1] Massachusetts Council of Churches, *Odyssey toward Unity*, Boston, MA, 1977. Ch. V, "Marks of a Truly Ecumenical Body", pp.41-49.

[2] *Baptism, Eucharist and Ministry*, Faith and Order Paper no. 111, Geneva, WCC, 1982, p.20, 1.5. See also the Vatican II Decree on Ecumenism, ch. 115.

[3] Massachusetts Council of Churches, *Ecumenical Accountability: What Are Our Responsibilities to and for Each Other?*, 1990, p.10.

[4] *Seventh Report of the Joint Working Group between the Roman Catholic Church and the World Council of Churches*, Geneva-Rome, 1998, pp.31-42.

6. Should Councils Become Interfaith?*

These days, hardly a meeting of a council of churches goes by without someone raising the question, "Should ecumenical councils of churches become interfaith bodies?" Often, this is not simply a theoretical issue. Rather, board members may be locked in a vigorous debate about whether or not they will change their own mandate and membership.

In many cases, the final vote is for a change. We have some serious concerns about the trend.

Although the Greek work *oikoumene,* from which the term "ecumenical" springs, means "the whole inhabited earth", early in this century "ecumenical" began to be used to apply to various forms of the Christian unity movement. These expressions of the ecumenical movement – councils of churches, interchurch dialogues, covenantal agreements, and so on – are committed to healing the divisions among the Christian churches for the sake of the world. Many continue to use the term in this manner, and to reserve "interfaith" or "inter-religious" for efforts to promote understanding and cooperation among different religious traditions (Jewish, Muslim, Buddhist, Hindu, etc.). This difference in terminology reflects a fundamental difference of purpose between the ecumenical and interfaith agendas.

Often, however, when an ecumenical organization becomes interfaith, a basic change in its purpose occurs, and all efforts to heal the still considerable divisions among the Christian churches are lost. What this redefined purpose is depends on the stated intentions of its members. It may include interfaith dialogue to reduce stereotypes and promote understanding. It may involve cooperation on projects of concern in the community, for example, organizing and staffing a shelter for the homeless or a feeding programme for the poor. It may cover planning for an interfaith worship

*The essay "Ecumenical or Interfaith? A Fresh Look at a Controversial Issue" first appeared in *The Living Light,* 1993, © 1993 United States Catholic Conference, Inc., Washington, DC, used with permission. The text also appeared in *Mid-Stream,* vol. 32, no. 4, Oct. 1993, titled "New Angles in a Lively Debate: Should Ecumenical Organizations Be Christian or Interfaith?", pp.31-40, used with permission.

service at Thanksgiving, or other special occasions. It may not even entail membership by interfaith bodies, but rather signal an intention to be open to such participation.

The configuration will depend on the context. A small, relatively homogeneous community with ten Christian churches and one or two Jewish synagogues whose council of churches "goes interfaith" will develop an agenda which may look considerably different from an organization in an urban area with rich religious diversity.

The underlying assumptions, however, are distinct from those of the Christian unity movement, whose official documents have said: (1) that the final aim of dialogue among churches should be to heal their divisions; (2) that cooperation is insufficient, and that cohesion is the goal; (3) that the Lord's table should be open to all Christians; and (4) that the celebrants at the supper should be recognized by all.

When discussed in a local context, the ecumenical/interfaith debate often gets aired from a pragmatic perspective. It focuses on what religious bodies can *do* together. This, in itself, is not an improper question, but it can be answered in other ways which do not undermine the ecumenical agenda.

Because other issues are involved, however, some prior questions may help sharpen the discussion. *On what basis* will we frame the ecumenical/interfaith organizational debate? What are the foundational issues on which we will rest our reasons?

Three reasons which often surface focus on the particular situation, a desire for inclusiveness, and good will. Perhaps concerns have arisen about problems among youth in the community. Because the difficulties affect everyone their resolution should involve everyone, and discussions about changing the organizational make-up of the council of churches emerge from the specific need. Or perhaps the town clergy association includes area rabbis – maybe also a local imam. The sense of cooperation and collegiality is strong, and some clergy begin to ask why this sense should not be extended to their congregations through the council. Or maybe council members begin to have a vague sense of discomfort about what appears to them to be an exclusive organization. These often seem to be the rationales which prompt the ecumenical/interfaith debate.

In contrast, three other concerns rarely are raised. These are key points that often are overlooked in making decisions about ecumenical/interfaith structures, and we believe that strong weight in this debate should be given to them.

1. The current state of ecumenical theology

Proposals to change organizational structures from an ecumenical to an interfaith intention prejudge answers to theological questions that have not been decided yet by the ecumenical church, and are in fact the topic of vigorous debate. Thus, such moves at this time are premature. They effectively decide issues before they have in fact been decided.

Some of the questions that surfaced at recent World Council of Churches' assemblies speak directly to these concerns. How inclusive can Christianity be of various cultural assumptions and practices before it violates its fundamental theological basis? What are the proper grounds for and what is the appropriate purpose of evangelization? Who is within the saving realm of God, and on what grounds do Christians base these claims? What is the purpose of the unity we seek for the churches, and why are we seeking it? How does that unity relate to the unity of all humankind, indeed of the cosmos?

A struggle is now going on within the ecumenical movement and within many of its member churches about the very meaning of the gospel. Is it truth, or is it simply a utilitarian tool – a useful vehicle for functioning in the world, without any ultimate claim to validity? On what grounds do we base our faith claims? How do we know these are valid?

A separate but related question is, if the gospel is culturally conditioned, as indeed all efforts to describe the divine must be in some ways, what are the limits to the intertwining of the two? At what point does the gospel become captive to culture? When do national identity and Christianity become

46

so interconnected that Christians no longer are free to critique culture?

These questions are as old as the gospel itself. Some of the early struggles that resulted in the development of Christian creeds were a result of these wrestlings. Our contemporaries saw these questions surface earlier in the 20th century with chilling force. The churches in Nazi Germany were confronted with stark challenges about their responsibilities in the face of a conflicting ideology. Out of this choice, the Confessing Church in Germany was born, the Barmen Declaration was crafted, and some said "no" to the dominant ethos.

Many of these questions take on a new sense of urgency today because we now are more *aware* than ever before that we live in a global village. How one community in that global village behaves often *affects* others. Our *self-interest* is at stake.

Thus, we feel a sense of urgency about these questions and an eagerness to answer them. We see our ecological interdependence. A nuclear disaster in Chernobyl affects the crops and livestock, for example, in Scandanavia and the United Kingdom. We are aware of ways that corporate mobility around the globe affects employment patterns and conditions for all. We are aware of the many potential reasons for conflict. Religion has been one of them, as it has been in Northern Ireland, the Balkans and many other places. We want to reduce religious differences, both among Christians and among people of many faiths, as a motive for destructive behaviour. And we are confused and in a quandary about how to do this.

It is tempting, in the face of these realities, to be too casual about the content of religious and ideological differences – to look for similarities and ignore differences, to gloss over distinctives and forget that they may result in concrete, practical problems. Christians should recognize, in addressing such differences, that we are dealing both with values and with truth. We may share some basic values with other world religions, but disagree about how we have come to hold the validity of these values. Those disagreements may, in fact, reflect some fundamental differences about the nature of divinity and humanity that result in problems as we implement our values. It is tempting, in our longing for justice, peace and the integrity of creation, to bypass the hard theoretical and practical work in which we and future generations must engage to help move closer to these goals. It is ironic that this temptation in interfaith dialogue is, in some ways, the exact opposite of what is happening in the ecumenical movement now, where churches seem to be championing their differences and forgetting that they theoretically are one in Christ.

We still must air fully these issues among our churches, and take seriously the concerns being raised. Until then, for historically ecumenical bodies with the stated intention of promoting Christian unity for the sake of the world (or, in the case of ecumenical professional organizations, with the intention of training and supporting those called to this vocation), to make such an organizational shift assumes answers to which we have not yet agreed within or among our churches. To make such a shift before we have greater clarity than now seems to be the case, in fact, functionally cuts off the debate.

2. Shared tradition

We must *go back to the texts* as the basis on which we frame this discussion. We need to explore the ecumenical consensus that has been developed thus far by the world churches involved in the ecumenical movement. The fundamental purpose of the ecumenical movement, according to documents honed by the gathered churches, is found in statements on the nature of the unity we seek developed by a series of World Council assemblies and Faith and Order gatherings.

A whirlwind tour of these texts reveals that the third world conference on Faith and Order in Lund, Sweden (1952), recognized that the practice of comparative ecclesiology which had been used in past ecumenical conversations was inadequate. In other words, discussions about different understandings of the nature of the church and its mission, with a contentment to leave the conversation in this state of "getting to know each other", was deemed insufficient. New attempts were made to move beyond comparisons to explorations of convergences and consensus when possible, and clarity about divergences when they exist. Lund recognized that one potential area of convergence is in common mission, and it focused on seeking unity in common mission. A key phrase in the Lund document says that "churches should do all things together which conscience does not compel them to do separately".

Picking up on the theme "Christ Is the Hope of the World", the World Council of Churches assembly in Evanston (1954) grounded our unity in Christ. This christological focus is the foundation, beginning, measure, from which we cannot stray. Using the phrase "all in each place", New Delhi (1961) concretized the vision. It suggested that every Christian in each locality (however defined) should be a visible part of the whole body of Christ, and that this unity should be shown in concrete ways.

Uppsala (1968) picked up an earlier theme, that unity does not imply uniformity, and developed the concept of catholicity as diverse, inclusive, and prefiguring the unity of humankind. We do not have to worship in exactly the same ways, or pray in the same ways, or be ordered in precisely the same ways, in order to live out the unity we have been given in Christ. Nairobi (1975) labelled the vision of New Delhi "conciliar fellowship", and built on its implications for local churches, envisioning "councils of representatives of all the local churches at various geographical levels to express their unity visibly in a common meeting". It also tried to respond to concerns and misperceptions emanating from earlier documents. Vancouver (1983) capitalized on the then recently completed text, *Baptism, Eucharist and Ministry,* and highlighted the eucharistic nature of the "fellowship" we seek. At the very least, our unity is rooted in our shared life through baptism in the name of the triune God; in our longed-for capacity to share the Lord's supper at the same table; and in a recognition that those called to ordination are ministers in the whole church of God in Christ. Canberra (1991) turned to the more encompassing concept of koinonia – community, communion – an idea mentioned in earlier documents, but used more fully in this latest effort. It also explicitly listed the four classical marks of the church – one, holy, catholic and apostolic – to describe the "church in its fullness".

This represents forty-one-plus years of shared labour in the ecumenical vineyard. We, as members of churches who have participated in this process, have a responsibility to pay attention to this fruit.

The quest for Christian unity for the sake of the world is not the only purpose of the church, nor is it the only purpose of individual Christians. It is, however, the primary purpose of the churches gathered together in the ecumenical move-ment, as they, and by implication, *we*, have thus far stated it. And in a reciprocal way, though councils of churches are not churches, unless they bear some marks of the church they are not doing their job properly, because councils are *of* the churches. They are shaped *by* them. They get their nature *from* them. Since structure proclaims intention ("the medium is the message"), to change the structure of ecumenical orga-nizations to interfaith bodies blurs and confuses our intention as churches in the quest for Christian unity.

3. The need for organizational collegiality

Ecumenical organizations at every level of church life have a responsibility to function collegially and accountably to each other *as organizations*. To abandon the ecumenical intention means that an organization formally (and almost always functionally) drops out of the ecumenical fold, and thus operates in isolation from the ecumenical church at all other levels.

Ecumenical organizations should mirror the sense of interconnectedness and inter-relationship among themselves which their members are seeking to embody. They are bound by their common purposes. A chief aim of a council of churches should be to cultivate an *ecumenical attitude* among all Christians and Christian churches within its boundaries. Councils should help people and churches understand the ecumenical vision, recognize it when they see it, long for it, appreciate it, celebrate it, cultivate it, identify resistances to it, want to overcome them, and work mightily to do so. In this way, councils of churches at every level share a common purpose. They should differ from each other because of the context in which they are functioning – international, national, regional, state or local. To the degree that they have a distinctive mission, it is derived from their distinctive context. Some means to achieve our common ends may be carried out better at different levels of church life. If we violate the shared ground-rules as they have been established thus far, we fail to "keep faith" with each other in essential ways.

How we can address interfaith concerns

For these reasons, we should resist moving from ecumenical to interfaith structures. Sometimes, the desire to "go interfaith" comes from an understandable interest in being fully inclusive of all religious expressions in a local community or among colleagues. We viscerally resist what feels to us like being an "exclusive club". Such feelings, though understandable, are not appropriate grounds on which to decide this issue.

And we do have alternative means at our disposal to address interfaith concerns, and respond to the reluctance to appear exclusive. We can be responsible to our mandate to exist "for the sake of the world", without making distorting organizational adjustments.

A variety of models for this alternative are now in practice. We can have an "interfaith desk", as now is the case both within denominations and in some ecumenical bodies. Whether responsibility is lodged in the hands of an individual or a committee, this approach can be one means to promote steady communication and facilitate regular cooperation among religious bodies, whenever opportunities make sense. Specific concerns, programmes and projects can be interfaith under the auspices of a conciliar organization. If a concern involves the whole community, the council can be a means for facilitating a community-wide response, without changing its structure or intention. Councils of churches can include interfaith dialogue as part of their programme. They can provide a means whereby representatives of all religious bodies come together over a sustained period to discuss practical and theoretical issues that divide and those that unite. When special tensions arise, the existence of an ongoing dialogue enables people to move more quickly and honestly to air core concerns.

Ecumenical professional organizations could include an "interfaith caucus", expressly for those persons whose organizations are inter-religious, but still try to maintain their ecumenical mandate alongside their interfaith membership. Such a caucus could help everyone address problems which are common to all similar organizations; it could explore ways in which bodies that are interfaith might help Christian members pursue the ecumenical agenda if no other vehicle in the community exists; and it could maintain its primary purpose of serving as a training ground for ecumenical leadership. This latter aim is especially important, since few means currently exist to help professional leaders of ecumenical organizations understand and interpret the theory and practice of the ecumenical movement.

In these ways, the ecumenical and interfaith agendas can be pursued without diminishing the aims of either. This is especially important for the Christian unity movement which is receiving criticism – some justified, some not – from many places these days, and which has a strong need to sharpen its self-understanding of purpose and goals.

If we take an honest look at church history, we must acknowledge that progress in the ecumenical movement is erratic and unpredictable. It comes in stops and starts, rather than a readily discernable, smooth, steady forward motion. So we may be tempted to give up on this rugged quest for Christian unity, and move to enticingly fresh interfaith terrain. That may be one of the underlying factors contributing to heightened local interest in interfaith relations. We feel that we've already "done" ecumenism, and now it is time to move on to new territory, which seems exciting because it is novel for many.

If we yield to this temptation, we will be abandoning the fundamental prayer of Christ "that they may all be one". This prayer, and the vision of unity reflected in the New Testament, is *rooted in the very being of God.* Christians confess the paradox of *unity* within the Trinity. They proclaim a God who so loved the world that God's only begotten Son was given in a redeeming, reconciling act. If we neglect the ecumenical mandate, we fail to be faithful to the full intention of God in Christ. If we neglect the ecumenical mandate, how can we with credibility and hope pursue our interfaith aims, however defined?

For these reasons, we hope ecumenical organizations will "keep the faith" – even when signs of success seem more like shadows than substance. We must trust that in God's own good time, the path will be made clear and the way plain.

7. Some Marks of Ecumenical Leadership

Almost every year new ecumenical professionals join the National Association of Ecumenical and Inter-religious Staff in the United States. From "old-timers" and newcomers alike, questions arise about how to do this job of conciliar administration. And whenever a council enters the search for a new director, similar questions are asked. What are we looking for?

The discussions often focus on techniques of successful fund-raising (are there any in ecumenical work?), necessary skills in addressing vexing personnel problems, ways to manage an unmanageable workload, or diplomatic methods to deal with religious leaders. The models we use often are from corporate managerial writings and these have much to teach anyone with administrative responsibilities.

Professional ecumenical leadership, however, challenges its practitioners to cultivate particular abilities *rooted in the ecumenical mandate itself, and refined by the unique nature of councils of churches.* When considering the role from this perspective, few if any ever succeed in achieving the ideal. If, however, we lack clarity about our aims, we might not even start walking in the right direction. What follows are suggestions aimed primarily at ecumenical professionals, yet they apply to everyone involved in the ecumenical enterprise.

First and foremost, ecumenical administration *is a form of ministry rooted in our baptism.* Leaders in the World Council of Churches are visibly reminded of this every time they walk into the chapel in the Ecumenical Centre. Crafted right into the floor are stream-like mosaic tiles, and above them on the wall hangs an icon of Jesus' baptism in the Jordan. Whether we are ordained or lay, we have been united with Christ and Christ's people through this act of incorporation. Barriers are transcended.

By thinking in these terms, the ecumenist brings to self-conscious focus a vision of catholicity, of wholeness, which forms and shapes his/her ministry. We claim all Christians as part of the family in this real though imperfect communion we share – whether they think so or not. We are claimed by them as belonging to their households, whether they understand this or not. This is the basis from which we begin.

Ministry is rooted in the church and ecumenical ministry belongs to the churches. Thus, we come to our calling from a particular tradition in a specific church. Yet we need to transcend those particularities, however imperfectly, even as we stay rooted in them, in order to be present to all. We need to understand, critically appreciate, and be involved in the church if we are going to work with the churches.

This attempt to hold our own tradition with open hands is an ideal expressed by the ecumenical movement and its leaders. Often, however, people find it hard to put this concept into practice. If ecumenical professionals learn to do this, and can be seen doing it, they model by example a vital element in the quest for Christian unity. Ecumenical leaders should, insofar as possible, embody an ecumenical spirit. In the words of that great American baseball player/ "philosopher" Yogi Berra, "You can observe a lot by looking."

What, then, are the marks of good ecumenical leadership? They involve an interweaving of personal, relational and communal skills.

1. An understanding of and appreciation for the ecumenical tradition

Echoing the words of Gabriel Fackre, we have to get the story straight before we can get the story out. Because councils of churches are peopled mostly by volunteer representatives who move into and out of their responsibilities relatively frequently, conciliar leaders are constantly in the process of helping new delegates understand the ecumenical history and vision from local and global perspectives. We have captured these ideas in print – far too much print! Unless, however, the texts are communicated by people they are often forgotten in dusty, disorganized archives.

If, on the other hand, the ideas are remembered collectively, they begin to take on some weight and life which transcend individuals. This is a systemic challenge. If the ecumenical professional does not recognize the need and does not help create structures to address it, transmission of the ecumenical tradition is far less likely to happen.

2. *The ability to understand, appreciate and interpret all Christian traditions*

A primary requirement for an ecumenist is curiosity. What makes us meet strangers or go into unfamiliar situations, beyond the fact that it is part of our ministry? We must have an insatiable desire to figure out why – why other people and churches think, believe, behave as they do. This very act of caring – of taking other people, churches and situations seriously, of communicating through our behaviour that they matter – is the beginning of breaking down what previously appeared to be insurmountable barriers. And in this process we are changed. Our horizons are expanded as we experience new ways of apprehending the gospel.

This, however, is only the first step. Ecumenical professionals take this new appreciation for the other and translate it so people and churches can approach others with fresh eyes.

3. *Tolerance for anxiety when faced with the unfamiliar: the ability to transcend it*

Not many people can walk into a room of difference and feel comfortable immediately. Whether you are the lone woman entering a room filled with male clerics, or a Protestant pastor attending an Orthodox dinner with robed and bearded priests, or a black professional in a dominantly white environment, you may feel an initial pang in the pit of your stomach.

Acknowledging this anxiety to God and to oneself is the beginning of its relief. The willingness to *ask questions* when one is uncertain, for example about matters of protocol, alerts others to our need. At the same time, this willingness communicates that we have taken others sufficiently seriously to ask. By this means, we learn. Bridges are built. The foreign becomes the familiar. Friendships are born.

4. A fondness for people – all kinds of people!

The late Cardinal Medeiros from the Archdiocese of Boston used to say he saw Christ in every person who walked into his room, but sometimes He was in such deep disguise! Retired Episcopal Bishop John Coburn talks about the way in which people are grace-bearers, and sometimes the people who get under our skin the most have the most to teach us – even if they are not aware of it and if what we learn is not what they intended!

Ecumenism is a people business. A capacity to appreciate people with all their brokenness and frailty and limitations is like sprinkling water on parched land.

5. A capacity to foster and respect participatory decision-making

Ecumenical work, by its very nature, is inefficient. It is so much easier to schedule a meeting if you do not have to consult fifteen denominational representatives about their schedules. It is so much easier to plan a programme if member churches are presented with a *fait accompli.* It is so much less work to prepare a common statement if the one denominational representative who always wants to change the text is not present for the drafting. This often is frustrating and exasperating. Unless we take time, however – and usually it takes a lot of time! – to include all members in a process, councils of churches are failing in one of our fundamental reasons for being, namely to be the churches together. We must respect both persons and processes. When we do so, we are able to experience a foretaste of the unity we seek.

6. An appreciation for the art of politics and diplomacy

At their best, these are lofty skills using appropriate means for valuable ends. Politics has acquired a bad name. People associate it with manipulation, dishonesty and self-interest – governments have no corner on this market. In its best sense, however, politics involves the proper use of authorized power for good ends. It involves devotion to duty; foresight in anticipating outcomes; the capacity to negotiate competing claims; sensitivity to feelings and concerns.

Willem Visser 't Hooft, the first general secretary of the World Council of Churches, was such a statesman. He would sit down with a church leader, perhaps over a cup of coffee, and listen. He would interpret. He would ask questions. He would repeat this process with other leaders until he could get a clear picture of a way through an impasse. Then he might craft a bit of language which might help everyone work their way through a problem and pull it out of his pocket at an appropriate point during a meeting. He listened, he created, and in so doing he facilitated.

Whether or not this is an idealized version of how he functioned, it offers an example to us all. The same problems, the human dynamics, the same stumbling blocks evidence themselves at every level of church life and call for the very best we have to offer in political acumen.

7. A willingness to delegate, empower, appreciate, thank

This is harder than it sounds, even if one subscribes to the values and is predisposed in this direction. Representatives to councils of churches often have multiple responsibilities, and their level of commitment to the ecumenical task may vary. So may their level of understanding. Even if people have a commitment, they may lack time. Thus, translating theory into practice is a challenge. Nevertheless, since councils of churches *are* their members, unless their representatives work together on a common task half the purpose of doing it is lost.

A conciliar professional is a bit like a cheer-leader. He or she functions as an energizer: cheers people on to the appointed goal, encourages them when the way seems hard, helps everyone celebrate when something is accomplished, and even occasionally enables people to have fun. This celebration of life and life together is renewing and entirely consistent with the spirit of thanksgiving which is gospel-rooted.

8. A commitment to accountability

Ecumenical leaders are accountable to their members. Ecumenical representatives – officially designated volunteers who serve in a variety of roles – are accountable to each other and to the council as a whole. This means they have a liaison function – reporting to and from the body. They must be well respected by the sending church in order to be fully effective ecumenical advocates.

9. The capacity to apologize

We aren't perfect. No one is. If we recognize it *before* anyone else, and in a spirit of humility acknowledge our weaknesses and our failings, we can become an endearing rather than alienating presence in awkward situations. In addition, we model an essential element in the ecumenical enterprise for all involved in it.

10. The ability to think systemically

If a plan or programme permanently changes the way churches think and act, then that plan affects not only the individuals involved but also their churches well into the future. Systemic changes can have positive or negative con-sequences for the ecumenical mandate. Ecumenical leaders need to be vigilant about the impact of such changes on the quest for Christian unity, and to look for positive initiatives which can mould structures.

Suppose, for example, that as a matter of policy churches decided that they would not ordain clergy unless the clergy demonstrated a knowledge of and appreciation for the ecumenical movement. This would have a positive ripple effect throughout the churches, producing systemic changes. Or suppose that a council of churches decided to offer regular, periodic courses in the history, theory and practice of ecumenism, and to enlist the churches as "partners" in this enterprise, responsible for recruiting and funding at least one student from each church. Over a period of time, the process would create a new cadre of ecumenical leaders who could "seed" ecumenical life in their area. These are examples of the process of thinking systemically, and producing changes which are more than ephemeral.

11. Charismatic authority

Council of churches executives are not bishops or "bishop-types". They are religious leaders, chosen by the member churches for a single purpose. They are called to be ecumenical advocates; to keep the mandate for Christian unity and mission before churches and their leaders; to help churches see the way forward; to cajole when necessary; to praise when possible; to be patient and impatient at the same time. They cannot do this unless they are respected.

In theory, when churches choose someone to fill the office of ecumenical leader, they are saying that they *want* that person to serve in this way. In practice, the authority of the office is fragile and easily eroded.

The authority of professional ecumenical leaders is largely charismatic. In other words, the person in the office must claim it for him- or herself and function in such a way to command respect. Only to a limited extent is the authority passed to succeeding leaders. This puts a heavy burden on anyone occupying the office.

One of the major temptations of ecumenical professionals, perhaps in their effort to exercise charismatic leadership, is to put themselves forward at the expense of the leaders of member churches and other elected representatives of the council. Keeping a balance is a difficult but necessary task.

12. The capacity to see over and interpret the whole picture

Council of churches leaders exercise a peculiar form of oversight which is an overview. Their members tend to see the ecumenical picture most clearly from their own vantage point, their own tradition, their own problems, their own strengths. If they understand other churches, usually it is with far less clarity and charity than their own.

This came home clearly to us recently when a group of Protestant and Orthodox religious leaders were meeting with editorial officials of a large regional newspaper. One Protestant member of the group spoke about a particular trend using the term "we". He assumed that his experience was universal to the delegation. In fact, not only did this inappropriately represent the Orthodox, but also his statement had a pecularly denominational flavour – a fact of which he was blissfully unaware.

Ecumenical leaders make it their business to understand all the Christian traditions their ministries encompass, to interpret these to other churches, and to remind everyone of the way in which they need each other in order to achieve a Catholic vision.

13. Cultivation of a healthy, mature spiritual life

As the Groupe des Dombes observed, a personal relationship with God is where the commitment to unity begins, where it is maintained, and how it is led. Without it, our appeals ring shallow. We lack bread for the journey. We grow impatient unless we realize that our ministries are rooted in God's time, not our own.

14. The ability to tolerate loneliness and to create community

Ecumenical ministry can be isolating. We must be rooted in our own church, yet claim and be claimed by all churches. Our vocation requires that we call into question the zealous loyalties of a particular church or tradition. This may be interpreted as disloyal.

The community we live in is so broad that it can be ephemeral. The staff of most ecumenical agencies is very small – often a single person. Few people will tell you to take care of yourself. Few, if any, will notice if you spend all those extra hours working. Few will tell you that you've done a good job. You can get burned out if you do not assume responsibility for taking care of yourself, and create a small community of friends and colleagues who can provide support, encouragement and counsel.

Periodic gatherings of professionals may offer some help. These may include regional or national meetings of colleague groups such as the National Association of Ecumenical and Inter-religious Staff, in the United States the newly developed annual gathering of state council of churches executives, similar regional retreats, or meetings of professional colleagues within an area.

15. A thick skin

We ask and expect a great deal of ecumenical leaders. The job, of necessity, requires multi-skilled individuals. In any single day, an ecumenical executive may have to negotiate a problem electric bill, solve a personnel difficulty, prepare and give a speech or sermon, offer live commentary in response to an inquiry from a radio commentator, answer correspondence (and now, faxes and e-mails!), staff or chair a committee meeting, discuss a diplomatic issue with a religious leader, and write copy for the council newsletter.

No single individual can do all these things equally well. No one is going to approach all his or her responsibilities with the same zest. And not everyone is going to give the ecumenical professional high favourability ratings all the time. The more inner-directed one can become, the more content one will be with one's ecumenical vocation – most of the time!

16. Patience, and plenty of it

An ecumenical professional recently returned from his holiday and said he had spent much of it repainting his living-room. When a colleague responded that this sounded more like work than vacation he replied that, unlike ecumenical work, you actually could see the progress of your painting and celebrate the visible fruit of your labours.

He was right. Ecumenical work is, of necessity, inefficient. If you are working together to change legislation of concern to member churches, it may take several years before a bill gets passed or defeated, and then you may not be sure how much of your collective effort contributed to the result. Negotiations to heal divisions among churches can take thirty years or more, and then require a return to the table if one church raises questions about the results. Some people labour for whole generations without seeing positive changes.

We have to remind ourselves that we are in this to be faithful, not necessarily successful, and to keep on keeping on.

All these marks of ecumenical leadership enable us to be *effective advocates for Christian unity.* We take the vision of wholeness which God has set before us – wholeness for the church and the world – and proclaim it on behalf of the churches who have called us to this specialized ministry. That is our call. That is our mandate. That is our burden and our joy.

8. Spirituality and Ecumenism

Ecumenism deals with healing relationships – between Christians, among churches, for the sake of the world. Christian spirituality deals with a relationship – to the triune God we know through Jesus Christ, and through God to each other. Because of their mandate, councils of churches are involved in fostering both of these relationships. In fact, if councils do not ground their ministry in this dual claim, they risk a loss of meaning and focus.

Through ecumenism and spirituality, we recognize that all too often our relationships with each other, indeed with the whole created order and thus with God, are broken and in need of mending. A loving God beckons us to the Godhead and to our neighbours.

Christians confess that God works through reconciling encounters. Part of the challenge of Christian spirituality is recognizing and responding to such signs of God's presence, God's activity and God's will. When we do, we find ourselves drawn to a reconciling Spirit that is at the heart of the ecumenical movement. Councils of churches and their leaders are in a special position to model and foster a healthy spirituality for ecumenism.

The words "ecumenism" and "spirituality" are often used indiscriminately. An ecumenical colleague once heard an inter-racial boxing match referred to as "an ecumenical bout". The word spirituality suffers from similar carelessness. The term is used to cover anything vaguely otherworldly. So when one writes about "ecumenical spirituality", the danger of sliding into sloppy definitions increases exponentially.

In an effort to steer through these murky waters, we want to define terms at the outset. Christian spirituality is the process of personal preparation that readies us to respond to God's initiatives, to discern God's activity. Through this process, by the grace of God, we may grow in understanding God, seeking closeness to or communion with God, and following the will of God in our life as it is lived in the community of the church and in society. Prayer is a traditional, primary means to praise, hear and respond to God. Prayer, however, is not the only means. Christians have relied on a variety of personal and communal ways to seek God, to receive God, and to do God's will. Ecumenism is the healing of divisions among Christian churches for the sake of the world.

Ecumenical spirituality and its forms

Thus, ecumenical spirituality encompasses all the attempts of Christians and Christian churches to approach the beckoning, reconciling God we know in Jesus Christ through the Holy Spirit; to listen to God's will in the various ways it is conveyed to us, with particular attention to what this means for divided Christians and their churches; to respond to God's call in our own behaviour and as we live together in Christian community in this reconciling spirit; and to attend to the ways that God beckons us to bring this reconciling spirit into the world. Ecumenical spirituality should provide the grounding and the environment in which we pursue the quest for Christian unity. This is at the heart of what it means to be the church, and thus of what it means to be churches together through instruments we call councils of churches. It is a distinctive set of keys for discernment.

Ecumenical spirituality deals with theology, because the quest for God implies a certain understanding of the nature of God as healing, reconciling, just and loving. It deals with ethics, because the struggle to know and do the will of God forces us to wrestle with concepts of morality and justice. It goads us to examine the ways in which our behaviours are corrosive to the human spirit, undermine right relationships, and erode human community in church and world. Ecumenical spirituality draws us into issues of ecclesiology, because assumptions about the church and its ministry sometimes exacerbate our divisions, and sometimes enrich the whole through our diverse understandings. It prompts us to consider liturgy, because our spirituality is shaped by sacramental assumptions with the power to divide or unite. Ecumenical spirituality touches the field of history. Our traditions and the memories we hold continue to influence our relationships and provide keys to unravelling past problems. It entails biblical studies, because hearing and studying the word together as it calls us to unity can be a source for spiritual meditation and growth. Ecumenical spirituality touches all these fields. Yet it is distinct, with its own focus.

The *forms* of ecumenical spirituality are consistent with the *means* Christians have used to be open to God and to do this together. Some of these include prayer, scripture reading, meditation (the pondering of the texts read), giving and hearing sermons, composition and singing of hymns, and worship. They appropriately are called "ecumenical" when their *intention* is consistent with the aims of ecumenism. Councils of churches can foster a range of programmes which involve these forms – ecumenical prayer services, ecumenical Bible studies, pulpit exchange programmes, ecumenical hymn sings, a celebration of hymns for unity, ecumenical retreats, and a variety of worship services.

An ecumenical spirituality makes certain faith claims. How Christians understand the nature of God as revealed in the life, death and resurrection of Jesus Christ has everything to do with how Christians understand themselves and the world around them. A beckoning, forgiving, healing, redeeming, righteous, reconciling, compassionate God draws us to Godself and to each other in this same Spirit. Thus, all efforts to foster community, heal brokenness, live with integrity and redress injustice are consistent with God's nature and intention.

Christian faith is incarnational. We confess that God acts in history. Furthermore, God comes to us in human flesh, through God's Son, in a unique way. God's Holy Spirit continues to work through us, in the life of the church and in the world.

Tradition and transformation

These basic assumptions about God and Christ have implications for ecumenical spirituality. We expect to see signs of God's presence in the created order, in the church and in human beings. We look for such signs. Furthermore, we know from the testimony of Christians through the ages that God does not always give us glimpses of Godself in predictable places. Thus, we have been schooled to be attentive to the unfamiliar, the unanticipated, even the unlovable (from our limited vantage point). The doctrine of the incarnation draws us to this perspective, so necessary for the ecumenical vocation.

Christian Tradition is a major means of conveying the significance of God's disclosures through the generations. Tradition involves not only authoritative teachings, but also dynamic teachers. All Christian churches have been blessed with spiritual leaders who have shed light on the journey of faith. The ecumenical movement enables Christians in all times and places to be enriched by the diversity of these spiritual witnesses.

One of the ironies of Christian Tradition is the idea that change is one of the ways in which God works. God is ever-transforming. The Holy Spirit is at work in the world. In an essay on ecumenical spirituality, Emmanuel Sullivan, SA, develops the implications of this idea for the ecumenical movement:

> Recognition must be given to the continuing activity of the Holy Spirit over long periods of separation among churches. Such recognition leads to a mutual evaluation and appreciation of particular spiritual gifts and practices found in various churches and Christian communities. Such traditions are acknowledged as gifts preserved or bestowed by the Spirit. As various Christian churches sought to reform and renew themselves in fidelity to the gospel, the Holy Spirit granted certain valid insights and spiritual gifts proper to authentic Christian life. Subject to spiritual discernment, such gifts and insights may well be intended for the future life of a visibly united church. Spiritual ecumenism respects the work of the Spirit uniting God's people in a diversity of gifts and ministries.[1]

Thus, we are called to be modest in our truth claims, aware that new light may be shed on God's word and will, some of which may come through the diversity in and among Christian churches.

Ecumenists who are attentive to the classic spiritual disciplines, prayer chief among them, over time often experience a certain fruitfulness in the quest for unity. When we offer to God in prayer our honest thoughts and feelings about our ecumenical experiences, God takes this raw material and uses it for God's reconciling intentions. Ecumenical leaders have opportunities to model this way of being and doing, and to bring the energy and creativity into their organizations.

Philip Sheldrake, author of *Images of Holiness,* describes what happens in this process. He says "contemplation is such a vital activity, for it is there where time and eternity, the particular and the universal intersect that we can recognize this God-given oneness as a prelude to recovering visible unity. Contemplation offers the possibility of a wholeness of vision that means we need no longer be cut off from large parts of our collective Christian inheritance but rather have access to all."[2]

For example, each of us often has been invited as a Protestant ecumenical guest at Roman Catholic and Orthodox eucharistic services. We love the liturgies. Often we are friends of the celebrants and many in the congregation. We participate as fully as possible in worship, until the distribution of the communion elements, which we as Protestants may not receive according to the discipline of these churches. At this point in the service, all of us are reminded painfully of the power of our remaining divisions.

Our pain has increased over the years. So has our fervent prayer for Christian unity – prayer we silently offer during distribution of the communion elements. The effect of these experiences has been to increase our zeal for the ecumenical task. We have discovered that God uses this pain as a witness to the scandal of our divisions and as a goad to heal them. The channelling of pain into constructive paths is a mark of a fruitful ecumenical spirituality.

On other occasions, usually in intimate gatherings among friends where our actions are understood and do not scandalize the faithful, the eucharistic rules get bent. This is a foretaste of the time when divisions among our churches will be healed. It is blessed food for the journey.

The power of the unfamiliar

Although ecumenical friendships are a gift of grace on the way, ecumenical encounters just as often plunge us into the unfamiliar – unfamiliar people, whose styles of worship, cultures, languages, beliefs and customs are different from our own. This can be disorienting, anxiety-producing and challenging. When councils of churches plan events involving people new to the ecumenical experience, we need to factor in this phenomenon, to give people permission to acknowledge it, and to help them move beyond it.

Each of us has experienced the charismatic fervour of some worship services – quite different from our Congregational and Disciples traditions. The Holy Spirit careens around the sanctuary in rolling waves of unbridled emotion, and on first encounter it is hard to know what to do with all that passion for God. After initial experiences, however, we have been able to anticipate what might happen. This has enabled us to relax, and to discover untapped emotional depths of prayer and praise we did not know were there.

In this way, ecumenical encounters, many of which can be planned intentionally by councils of churches, deepen and broaden our spirituality. They enhance our appreciation for the diversity of spiritual traditions. If we give these initially unfamiliar experiences a chance, they enrich our capacities for worship and human relationships.

Like latter-day Abrahams and Sarahs, we must be willing to venture into strange lands to encounter afresh the living God, and to jar us out of our fixed ways. In this process, we become open to new ways of seeing what God wants us to see. We must be willing to endure the uncomfortable if we are going to grow. This, in itself, is a spiritual discipline.

In an oft-quoted sentence from Vatican II's *Decree on Ecumenism,* we read that "there is no ecumenism worthy of the name without a change of heart". This statement shows an intriguing convergence between contemporary Roman Catholic and Protestant thinking about the spiritual concept of conversion and its implications for Christian unity. When we venture into the ecumenical arena, we and our churches must be open to the possibility of conversion – a turning away from sin, a reorientation towards God, and a transformation of our relationships with each other and in society. In this process, we are drawn to conform our hearts more closely to the heart of God we know through Jesus Christ.

When we allow our hearts to change, we may also find ourselves listening more openly to those who are different. We may evidence a quality of catholicity, of inclusiveness, of bringing others into the circle, of mentoring new generations of leaders. This catholic spirit is an essential aid in discerning the work and will of God. When we listen to those who are different, we see with new eyes.

This inclusive spirit is in imitation of Christ. He gathered disciples from all walks of life, with different personalities and temperaments, strengths and weaknesses, political and economic backgrounds. Their unity was in the God they came to know through Jesus Christ, not necessarily in their natural affinities towards each other. This quality of inclusiveness may stretch us beyond our inclinations. We can get wearied by theological, liturgical and cultural diversity. It takes more time and energy to understand people who are unfamiliar. And yet by widening our perception of the Christian circle, God brings renewal.

Humility is a precondition for catholicity. It is also a fruit of a healthy spiritual life. Humility is an active virtue demanding repeated self-examination. Our pilgrimage as individuals and as churches is a living, growing thing. It is not a static achievement, once accomplished, never in need of reform. The life of holiness is one of movement, process, imperfection, failure, longing, healing, searching for God and for each other. Personal and corporate humility are necessary components in a full spiritual life and in responsible ecumenical engagement.

The power of Christian hope

Another dimension of the change of heart to which we are called is in the realm of the material world. Contemporary writing on Christian spirituality has drawn from the sciences and benefited from a broader understanding of the human psyche. Thus we see an integral relationship between our bodies and our souls. We see the connections between the material and the spiritual realms. This holistic view of human nature, and of our relationship to and interdependence with the whole created order – all of which are of God – pushes us to take seriously the need for the material well-being of our brothers and sisters. As Sheldrake has observed, "injustice denies the presence of God in the other and is thus a form of practical atheism".[3] Thus, the World Council of Churches' focus on "justice, peace and the integrity of creation" is directly connected to ecumenical spirituality.

As we move into the 21st century, many of us have become so accustomed to making judicious assessments of the calculated possibilities for measured movements towards unity that we have lost the capacity for Christian hope. We keep trying to trim God's reconciling mandate down to our limited imaginings, as a whole range of articles describing an "ecumenical winter" illustrate; but the vision of Christian unity God has put before us is expansive. Big dreams call for big hopes.

This is solid Christian theology. It rests on the promises of God. In response to these promises, we need to get down on our knees or up on our feet in prayer, and we need to be doing it together. Those gathered for the World Council of Churches' Evanston assembly in 1954 said: "The measure of our concern for unity is the degree to which we pray for it. We cannot expect God to give us unity unless we prepare ourselves to receive his gift by costly and purifying prayer. To pray *together* is to be drawn together." When we ground our daily lives as individuals and as churches in the spiritual disciplines, we open ourselves to the transforming work of the Holy Spirit. We create space where we can allow greater coherence between what we say we believe about the church and how we behave as its members. As the early Christians discovered on Pentecost, when the Holy Spirit gets moving, extraordinary things can happen.

The ecumenical movement needs people with a Christlike frame of mind. We are one *in Christ*. We are called to conform ourselves *to Christ.* We seek the mind *of Christ.* We see the church as the *body of Christ.*

Attention to the spiritual dimension of our ecumenical vocation fosters this Christ-like frame of mind. It widens our vision. It transforms individuals and churches.

Sometimes we may be overwhelmed by the enormous gap between where we are and where Christ beckons us to be. The problems seem intractable. The pain of our divisions feels overwhelming. Frustrations build.

All such experiences are the raw material of prayer. We should be able to bring our concerns before God – both alone and together. Being faithful ecumenists sometimes means just going on being faithful.

A survey of the history of the ecumenical movement reveals how whole generations of Christians laboured for unity and saw little fruit. Then another generation came and took a quantum leap because of all that had gone on before. Ecumenical progress comes in jerky lunges rather than in a steady forward progression. It entails struggle – a necessary part of authentic discipleship. If this is of God, we should do what we can where we are, and trust that it will bear fruit in God's good time.[4]

NOTES

[1] Emmanuel Sullivan, SA, "Ecumenical Spirituality", in *The Westminster Dictionary of Christian Spirituality,* Gordon S. Wakefield, ed., Philadelphia, Westminster, 1983, p.126.

[2] Philip Sheldrake, *Images of Holiness: Explorations in Contemporary Spirituality,* London, Darton, Longman & Todd, 1987, p.14.

[3] *Ibid.,* p.17.

[4] Portions of this chapter also appear in *The Vision of Christian Unity: Essays in Honor of Paul A. Crow, Jr,* Thomas F. Best and Theodore J. Nottingham eds (Indianapolis, Oikoumene Publications, 1997. Used with permission.

9. Challenges and Dangers

In the course of any day, the phone in a council of churches office rings a great deal. Incoming calls – or these days, faxes and e-mails – give a glimpse of the challenges faced by these ecumenical bodies. A twenty-something prospective bride wants to know if there is a beautiful chapel within a ten-block radius of the scheduled location of the wedding reception. A newspaper reporter asks for a comment about the legislature's refusal to open liquor stores on Sundays. A denominational staff person calls to suggest that the council host a programme about domestic violence, since the topic is of concern to all the churches and none of them has time to handle the project themselves. The electrician wants to schedule a time when he can repair the wiring in the office so the copying machine will work properly. A church secretary phones to ask if a representative can be present for the annual fall mission fair – a way for the church benevolence committee to determine its mission giving for the following year. A newly graduated seminarian wants to talk with the council director about job prospects. A church advocacy group sends an e-mail asking for immediate help with a particular senator on election law reform. An ecumenical officer calls to ask if the council can help organize a forum on responses to the papal encyclical *Ut Unum Sint* (That All May Be One). And so it goes. In the face of these competing demands and the assumptions that underly them, professional and volunteer leaders in councils of churches face several fundamental challenges:

1) focusing on their basic purpose and goals, to avoid dissipating energies;
2) communicating these goals effectively to the uninformed and unconvinced;
3) dealing efficiently with the tasks of institutional maintenance that undergird loftier aims;
4) enabling genuine movement in the face of manifold resistances; and
5) sustaining these practices through evolving generations of volunteer and professional ecumenical leadership.

It isn't easy.

Finances

Many of the difficulties that councils experience are rooted in the problems of the member churches. If finances in the churches are tight, the churches may cut council funding first. "Treat us as you treat yourselves," some conciliar leaders have said appropriately. "We have no right to expect more. We should not have to expect less." If staff salaries are level-funded, it is understandable and fair that a church's membership grant to the council stay the same. If, however, the church staff receives a 4 percent increase, it is appropriate and fair that the membership grant to the council should be increased by the same amount.

Note the term "membership grant". Member churches tend to think of their internal expenses as obligations, their financial offerings to councils as gifts – contributions out of their excess, adjustable based on internal circumstance. Yet if the ecumenical mandate is inherent in the gospel, and therefore an essential aspect of the *being* of the church, this theory should be reflected in practice – *all* practice, including the budget. In some parts of the two-thirds world financing ecumenical endeavours poses daunting challenges which defy simple answers. Latin American ecumenical leaders have bemoaned "the steady decrease in the financial resources available for ecumenical work". In a gathering focused on finances, they said: "This situation jeopardizes the continuity of ecumenical actions and hence our possibilities and opportunities for contributing actively to changing the conditions of exclusion, injustice, discrimination and suffering which have such grave repercussions on the lives of our peoples, individually and collectively."[1] Underlying the budgetary pressures of councils and their members are the sweeping sociological changes in main-stream denominations which are the backbone of council membership in the North American and European scene. As church memberships remain static or shrink, the religious landscape may be shifting in ways that are definitive. At this juncture councils face a particular temptation to seek significant funding from outside sources in order to sustain programmes. If they succeed, they may continue their programmes but lose their ecclesial roots. In so doing, they cease to be what they proclaim – a council *of* the churches. If they fail, they may keep their integrity but lose their existence! The choice is brutal.

All of this presumes that the people making decisions about such matters understand the ecumenical mandate and are committed to it. They often do not and are not. This points to another problem for councils – lack of ecumenical formation. Those designated to serve on boards and committees and even on the staff of councils may have an ecumenical inclination but they probably do not have an ecumenical education. This problem is compounded by the sheer scope of diversity often represented around the ecumenical table, and the complexity of issues underlying our divisions. This can be quite intimidating to a newcomer.

Training and tradition

Seminaries and churches have been lax in providing training about ecumenical theory and practice. They assume that exposure to people of other religious traditions is adequate. It is not. Councils should continue to hold their member churches and their educational institutions to account. They could, for example, recommend that a periodic audit be conducted to assess curricula for ecumenical offerings. Given competing pressures on Christian education, however, a more fruitful approach to the problem may be for churches to address the need *together* through the council. Together they could offer occasional courses (with particular focus on the relationship between the local and the universal ecumenical situation). Six New England state councils of churches in the US have banded together to co-sponsor what they call the Ecumenical Institute of New England — offering, on an annual rotating basis, eighteen hours of instruction on the history, theory and practice of the ecumenical movement. Councils could provide scholarships to students for off-site training at places such as the World Council of Churches' Ecumenical Institute at Bossey near Geneva, and the Centro Pro Unione of the Atonement Friars in Rome, assume responsibility for seminary interns, and look for other creative ways to mentor new generations of ecumenical leaders. Councils also can use their own board and committee meetings as occasions for continuing ecumenical education.

A companion difficulty councils face is in finding ways to foster the ecumenical tradition – those means whereby the story of the churches' shared efforts can be built on by successive generations. Because professionals and volunteers often cycle relatively quickly through councils of churches, leaders of ecumenical bodies unwittingly may ignore the progress of their predecessors; or they may repeat approaches previously tried and found wanting.

Putting the story in writing can help. For example, a compiled collection of a council's public policy documents both provides ready access and gives a visual, visceral sweep to the ecumenical tradition churches have forged together over the years. Preparing a packet of materials for new board members with the obvious items – the constitution and by-laws, personnel policies, position statements, list of available resources, key texts, list of board and staff members with church affiliations and addresses, etc. – can help members get oriented and foster an understanding that they are a part of the communion of ecumenical saints who have laboured before them.

The importance of membership

This tendency towards a lack of understanding and appreciation by churches for the ecumenical aim of visible unity causes another problem for councils. They sometimes are seen as "mission agencies" – convenient and (perhaps) efficient venues for cooperation on matters that are perceived to be tangential to the survival of the churches, but nothing more. This lack of vision and commitment to deeper unity, with all the hard work entailed, can drag councils towards an ecclesially corrupt subservience, and sap them of vitality.

There are no easy answers to this recurring problem. Eternal vigilance by ecumenical leaders is essential, coupled with a vigorous dose of assertive ecumenical education when the occasion warrants!

Another challenge faced by denominational structures – and thus, by councils as well – is a suspicion of anything that smacks of bureaucracy. The current tendency by congregations to concentrate on that which can be seen, experienced and controlled in their own context puts denominational bodies at a distinct disadvantage. Councils of churches can be similarly handicapped, but even more so.

This problem is exacerbated when the member churches of a council do not make that membership evident to their constituencies. For example, if the quarterly denominational newspaper, which is sent free of charge to all churches and local church leaders, rarely if ever includes news about the things churches are doing together through the council, it will be difficult for the council to penetrate this wall of silence. Whether evolving new communications technologies help councils more effectively lift the fog of invisibility remains to be seen. Councils are able to mitigate this problem somewhat by sending their own communications to congregations. The word is attended more fully, however, if it is also shared through the sanctioning body.

Councils also have been able to counter the difficulties caused by invisibility by going directly to secular media on those occasions when they have something newsworthy to say. All this assumes, however, that they have the time, energy and expertise to take this approach – a tall order when councils are under-staffed (if staffed at all) and under-financed.

One of the most serious problems councils of churches now face is new forms of disagreement among members. This, too, is a challenge within member churches that also surfaces among them. The challenge to councils is even more threatening, however, because the ecumenical ties that bind the churches together are more tenuous than their own internal commitments. If churches leave the ecumenical table, they perceive fewer immediate internal consequences than if they leave their own ecclesial table.

Yet the churches themselves are strained, sometimes nearly to the breaking point, by disagreements over such issues as human sexuality, leadership, authority and governance, the relationships between men and women in the church, and inclusive language. One of the results of these tensions has been a tendency to avoid controversy in ecclesiastical gatherings. This approach smooths the minor irritations but leaves the major ones unmanaged. Like underground fires in dry tinder, they flare up out of control with unpredictable and often dire consequences.

Handling conflicts

How, in the face of these difficulties among churches involved in conciliar life, can the churches together handle conflicts that seem too terrifying to touch? There are no magic answers to this question, but some elements are essential. The aim of councils is the creation of a climate where visible unity among the churches can be realized, rendering councils obsolete. Short of that goal, churches together through a council should stay focused on the drive towards proximate unity on matters where this is possible, and on the will to discuss their differences responsibly and respectfully when it is not.

Unity does not always have to mean unanimity in all matters, any more than this is possible – or even desirable – in internal ecclesial deliberations. If councils were held to this strict policy, the churches together would be paralyzed and members would voice frustration that they never did anything significant. One church effectively could be given veto power over the whole body. The freedom of the Holy Spirit would be constrained.

On the other hand, part of an authentic discernment process is the respectful listening to all voices, including a minority of one, if necessary. The role of ecumenical leaders in such a situation is to continually call the churches and their representatives to this high standard of ecclesial behaviour, which is rooted in the common search for the mind of Christ.

A number of factors are necessary to foster this climate. (1) Ecumenical leaders must be trustworthy, and must be seen to be so. They cannot succumb to the temptation to manipulate a process, and they must challenge others who have the tendency to do so. (2) Ecumenical leaders should look for safe spaces in which controversial conversations may take place. Safe may mean small – for example, among a few religious leaders gathered in informal conversation, perhaps over a meal. Safe certainly initially means off the record, to encourage candour. Safe means respectful. People may get angry, but their anger must be expressed within certain honourable bounds. Safe probably means slow. Such processes cannot be rushed. (3) When difficult issues must be dealt with in large, public ecumenical contexts, people should pay as much attention to the process they will use to air their concerns as to the context of those concerns.

The ecumenical movement has emphasized repeatedly that our prophecy is strengthened by our unity. The credibility of our Christian witness is undermined when we are divided. This is one of the strong reasons why the ecumenical movement is so important. Even when churches disagree on particular issues, however, if we can disagree without division, if we can keep our fights within the Christian family, without causing further breaches in whatever minimal unity we already have been able to achieve, we will model more faithfully to the world around us the reconciling drive at the heart of the Christian gospel. One implication of the term "ecumenism" is that we can disagree vigorously about the truth on many fundamental issues, and make clear we disagree. We must do so, however, with the pre-eminent truth of reconciliation as our primary organizing and directing principle.

Most of the foregoing challenges exist within as well as among the churches. A few additional ones are particular to councils of churches and the ecumenical movement.

When there is not enough movement in matters ecumenical, when the pace is steady but slow, or when churches seem to regress rather than progress in their relationships with each other, people get discouraged. Americans especially live in the now. They expect instant gratification. Five years seems like an eternity. Yet many ecumenical conversations leading to substantively changed relationships have taken thirty years or more. Without this long view, without this historical sweep, people easily can lose heart. This tendency can be countered only with historical memory. When one knows a wide span of years and can look at them retrospectively, then one knows where progress has been achieved. Ecumenical leaders have a crucial role as keepers of memory. They also can identify signs of progress by seeing the small steps within the big picture, noting them, and helping people to celebrate along the way. They become, in effect, cheer-leaders for Christian unity – an essential but often overlooked role, specially when the cheer-leaders themselves may get discouraged. All of this is rooted in a healthy ecumenical spirituality.

Common worship

Agreeing on suitable common worship also is a challenge for councils. The very process of working out liturgies is an ecumenical education but not necessarily one for the faint of heart. Discussions about inclusive language and the dogmatic debates underlying it; the use of free form versus fixed prayers; which hymns to sing (if any); the role of confessional statements; who may serve as appropriate leaders; who can do what with whom! – all these issues and more surface when people plan ecumenical worship. Underlying these challenges is the pain of our inability to come to the same eucharistic table among Protestant, Roman Catholic and Orthodox churches – the greatest scandal of all, and a constant goad towards unity.

And yet, *not* to worship together is an unsatisfactory alternative. Fortunately, we have some help. A half century of international ecumenical gatherings has provided some guidance about commonly acceptable forms. These tend to be a little bit uncomfortable yet faintly familiar to most, and thus provide a workable guide. The Consultation on Common Texts has developed suggested services for common prayer, now being updated. Regular ecumenical occasions, such as the Week of Prayer for Christian Unity and the World Day of Prayer, offer suggested orders of worships which may be adapted to local situations.

The *process* of planning ecumenical worship may be as illuminating as the product, as long as ample time is provided for a representative group of people to work through the issues involved.

Perhaps the greatest challenge councils of churches face is the lack of will by their members. The status quo is a comfortable state – especially when churches are feeling threatened within and without. Yet when ecumenical leaders are able to voice the inextricable links between the mandate for unity and the nature of the church, they serve as prods towards progress. The quest for Christian unity always has been a minority movement within the church – a prophetic voice calling the churches to account for their divisions. And in the final analysis, our duty is to be faithful to this call. We can leave the success part to God.

NOTE

[1] *Economic Viability of the Ecumenical Movement in Latin America: From Dependence to Self-reliance,* Salvador, Bahia, Brazil, 24-27 Sept. 1996, Geneva, WCC, 1996, p.10.

10. The Future of the Ecumenical Movement

In chapters 2-9, we dealt specifically with councils of churches, raising issues that will confront councils for the foreseeable future, for example, the meaning of membership, the gifts needed for leadership, the relation of theory and practice, the problem of finances, and the need for effective communication. In this chapter, we return to the broader perspective found in chapter 1 by asking: What are the ten most pressing challenges that the ecumenical movement as a whole is likely to face in the coming years? Since councils are a key instrument of the movement, these challenges will almost certainly shape the life and agenda of conciliar bodies as they move into the 21st century.

1. One is *the challenge of maintaining effective, flexible and robust ecumenical structures*. Structures are never as important as the vision that calls them into being, but they are nonetheless important – as we have tried to suggest throughout this volume. Councils of churches will undoubtedly change in the years ahead (as they have in the past); but if the ecumenical movement is to move, then the churches that comprise it will need to come together in some organizational form in order to promote prayer, dialogue, advocacy, evangelism, social witness and cooperation.

As we write these pages, several high-profile councils of churches, including the national council in our own country, are in crisis and/or radical transformation. When facing such a situation, the question for the churches to ask is not "How do we keep this particular structure afloat?" but "What kind of organization is needed in this era and this place in order to live out our ecumenical mandate?" If this renewal movement called "ecumenical" is to have a future, then conciliar bodies will play a vital role.

2. *The challenge of relating the search for Christian unity to interfaith dialogue, without confusing the two:* We have already discussed this issue at some length in chapter 6. The challenge, as we suggested there, is to show that the two efforts are complementary while resisting the notion that Christian ecumenism is somehow passé in a religiously pluralistic world. God calls us both to reconciliation in the

human family and to koinonia (communion, sharing, mutual participation, fellowship) as followers of Christ. These are distinguishable goals with particular problems and methodologies; but they certainly are not "either-or".

3. *The challenge of keeping the various ecumenical efforts together in one coherent movement:* The genius of the modern ecumenical movement is in the attempt to integrate concern for unity, justice, mission, service, education and renewal in one overarching vision of church and world. To put it another way, the ecumenical vision resists the tendency to split doctrinal reconciliation from active commitment to justice – as if racism were not an ecclesiological issue or baptism had nothing to do with how we act justly in the world! This is a movement that says baptism, eucharist and ministry and the Programme to Combat Racism in the same breath. But living that out, especially in councils of churches, will continue to be a challenge.

There are other ways, of course, to divide the movement. "We're going to put our eggs in the basket of bilateral, theological dialogues and give less energy to councils." "We're interested in relationships with Roman Catholics but not with evangelicals." "We think the world and national councils are irrelevant to our situation, and so we'll just concentrate on local matters." Surely, in the perspective of the gospel, these are not alternatives. In our judgment, the failure to see ecumenism as a whole weakens every part of it.

4. *The challenge of preserving appropriate theological diversity while standing firmly against so-called diversities that are contrary to the gospel:* This has been a central (if not the central) dilemma for the ecumenical movement from its beginning, and the challenge will likely intensify in the years ahead. Christians now generally agree that the amount of water used in baptism is a secondary concern on which we can appropriately differ. Can the same be said, however, about the threefold ministry with bishops in apostolic succession? There is now a broad consensus that theological support for racial separation (apartheid) is a heresy which the church must stand and teach against if it is to be the church.

But what about support for the possible use of nuclear weapons? Is that an issue on which Christians can agree to disagree? In the United States, the state council of churches in Montana has issued a Declaration on Distortions of the Christian Gospel (1996) which repudiates as false the teachings of white supremacist groups that claim the name of Christ. It is a way of affirming that there are limits to the church's theological diversity, limits which the member communions (with all of their theological differences) must identify together for the sake of the good news.

There is a related issue that we should, at least, flag. Recent years have witnessed previously unimaginable convergence on such topics as sacraments, ministry, worship, authority, and the nature of the church as koinonia but, in a sense, this has simply cleared the decks of Reformation-era disputes. The question now is: What are the truly divisive issues of our era? The Baptist theologian Mark Heim has written that "the ecumenical movement needs to be reinvented in such a way that it is understood and owned as our primary effort and hope for addressing [this era's] most threatening divisions". We agree, but this is by no means easy! Councils of churches should be "safe places" where churches can learn to talk with one another honestly about truly difficult issues without their trust in, or commitment to, one another being weakened. At some point, however, they also need to speak together to the world.

5. *The challenge of affirming appropriate cultural diversity while also claiming our unity in Christ:* Over the past twenty years, the ecumenical movement, especially at the global level but also within countries, has become a dialogue of cultures every bit as much as it is a dialogue of confessions. This is tremendously enriching; but it also raises a new set of difficult issues. For example, Korean theologian Chung Kyun Kyung provoked great controversy at the WCC's assembly in 1991 when she made use of images from Korean Shamanism in order to reflect on the activity of the Holy Spirit. Is this legitimate contextualization or illegitimate syncretism? The debate will surely continue for years to come.

Perhaps the major challenge in this regard will be to preserve and revitalize the encounter between Christians of the West and Orthodox churches. Orthodoxy is a genuinely non-Western form of Christianity - which means, among other things, that it has not been shaped by the questions of modernity. In this post-cold war era, these cultural differences are now erupting into open dispute, creating real challenges for councils that include various church families.

6. *The challenge of challenging the ecclesiological assumptions of the churches:* This is another of those perennial problems, one that has particular importance for conciliar ecumenism. The issue we have in mind was nicely summarized by a former executive of the WCC: "Claiming churchliness for themselves alone, the denominations continue to deny to councils and other instruments of unity the ecclesial significance that would empower them to challenge the continuing separate existence of the denominations." A council of churches, as we have stressed, is not the church; but the very existence of a council should remind the denominations that they are not the church either – at least not the whole of it. How many times have we heard bishops or other judicatory leaders say, "Involvement in the council must be a secondary priority because my first responsibility is to 'the church'." But surely this is faulty ecclesiology. If one's responsibility is for leadership in the church, then involvement in ecumenical ministry should be part of the job description – but that is a challenge.

7. *The challenge of turning the results of ecumenical dialogue into new ways of living together locally:* This is the issue that ecumenists often call "reception" – "receiving" the gifts, including the gift of increasing unity, that the Spirit gives through the ecumenical movement. Recent decades have witnessed astonishing convergence on questions that once were cause for open hostility; but such convergence often has little impact on congregational life. Closing this gap will likely be a major focus of ecumenical concern for the next generation.

8. *The challenge of nurturing in a new generation of clergy and lay leaders a passion for ecumenism, and a vision*

of the churches' fullness: We think it is fair to say that seminaries, at least in Europe and North America, have not done an adequate job of forming a new generation of ministers who are ecumenically knowledgeable and committed. The ecumenical movement is no longer new or sexy; and besides, many seminaries seem to think they have fulfilled all righteousness by being interdenominational. The churches generally don't emphasize unity in their church school materials – because, after all, the ecumenical movement challenges denominational prerogatives. And the ecumenical student movement, which once exposed youth leaders to the joys and struggles of shared life, has lost much of its vitality. Thus, it is hard to overstate the urgency of this challenge.

9. *The challenge of expanding the circle of participants in the ecumenical movement:* This challenge really has two parts, one having to do with what might be called "human diversity" and one with "confessional diversity". With regard to the former, the ecumenical movement (painful to say) has often operated with a white, North Atlantic mind-set that has not felt at home to persons of colour. This is tricky, since numerous persons of colour are in positions of ecumenical leadership, especially at the global level. But the "traditional" church unity agenda is still widely perceived to be the province of white Westerners; and this hinders the integration of unity and justice outlined above.

The second half of this challenge is to expand the ecumenical tent to include those sisters and brothers in Christ whose churches have avoided the very word "ecumenical". Already, the member churches of the World Council of Churches represent only a quarter of the world's Christians, and that percentage will fade rapidly in the coming years.

One way of stating this concern is to repeat what we said above: that the ecumenical movement must be a place where the actual divisions of the church are fully, painfully present. Many of the old fissures associated with the years 451, 1054 and 1517 have been addressed to an amazing extent; but new divisions associated with such labels as "evangelical", "Pentecostal" and "conservative" should now be on the agenda.

The difficulty for councils will be to reach out to new partners without (a) weakening the bonds of fellowship that have already developed among the current members, and (b) weakening the justice commitments that are found on current agendas.

10. We have named the previous nine challenges in what we regard as ascending order of importance; although, to be honest, that order could easily be rearranged. We have no doubt, however, that *the most pressing challenge before us is the need to recover and proclaim with passionate conviction the gospel-based vision of reconciliation in Christ that has historically been at the heart of this movement*. This, of course, brings us back to chapter 1. The mandate for ecumenical work is the same in the year 2000 as it was in 1900 and will be in 2100: to bear witness to the God of peace and justice, the God made known to us in Jesus Christ, through the way we live with one another. It is from this conviction, this vision of wholeness in Christ, that the ecumenical movement gets its energy, purpose and direction.